Economics and the Real World

to Lisse,

with regards

+ love.

Cindy K.

Economics
and the Real World

ANDREW M. KAMARCK

University of Pennsylvania Press
Philadelphia

Published 1983 in the United States by the University of
Pennsylvania Press

First published 1983 in Great Britain by Basil Blackwell

Library of Congress Cataloging in Publication Data

Kamarck, Andrew M.
  Economics and the real world.
  Bibliography: p.
  1. Economics. I. Title.
HB71.K275 1983 330 83-10331
ISBN 0-8122-7902-6

Printed and bound in Great Britain

Contents

Preface   vii

1   Introduction   1

2   Problems of Measurement in General   8

3   Special Sources of Inaccuracy in Economic Data   12

4   Loose Concepts and Economics   21

5   National Income and Product Accounts   42

6   Balance of Payments   63

7   Macroeconomic Models   69

8   Microeconomics   80

9   Welfare Economics and Cost – Benefit Analysis   98

10   'Capital' and 'Investment' in Less Developed
     Countries   106

11   Operational Conclusions   117

Technical Appendix: Significant Digits   134

Bibliography   141

Index   157

Preface

[It is my]. . .belief that in the present period economics as a practical art is ahead of economics as a science. At this stage most of us prefer the advising of government economic policies entrusted to the experienced intuitive economist.

Koopmans, *Three Essays*

My work on this subject was provoked by certain aspects of my experience over the last 40 years. I learned that the economic analysis that is actually useful for guiding government decisions is fairly basic but highly effective when supplemented by good judgement derived from experience of how human beings and institutions react. I also found, as have many others, that in the last generation many young economists, fresh out of the university, are ill-equipped to confront the economic problems of the real world. The brightest of these, if they wish to be effective, learn to discard as useless or misleading much of what they have been rewarded in the university for learning. Some even become inclined to go too far and discard all they have learned as useless baggage.

The second main element stimulating this work was the failure of the attempt by Dr Virgilio Barco, one of the ablest of the World Bank's executive directors, to get the Bank to abandon spurious precision — for example, showing a country's GNP per capita to the nearest dollar when it was obvious that the margin of error in calculating GNP was very large. (The highly useful World Bank's *World Tables* is full of examples of this spurious precision. In the USA, the Bureau of the Census reports that the 1970 population census had an error of around 2½ per cent. In the *World Tables*, Ethiopia's population is given to the nearest hundred, with a relative error of 0.0002 per cent, or 10,000 times more precise than the US census even though Ethiopia has never had a complete census!)

Beginning with the presidential address of Wassily Leontief to the American Economic Association in 1970 (Leontief, 1971), several other presidents of economists' societies in the United Kingdom and the United States have over the years expressed dissatisfaction with the current relationship of economics to reality and reinforced me in my belief that research on this subject was overdue. It also became clear that it was useless to expect economists to change the common practice of the profession without their having a theoretical justification and practical guide for the change. Since no one else has appeared willing to undertake the task I have done so.

I have tried to make the paper as intelligible as possible in the hope that it will be read by non-economists who are consumers of economists' memoranda as well as by economists themselves. I have tried to avoid economists' jargon and technical language as much as I could in the text, but put in parenthetical remarks when fuller communication with economists seemed to demand it.

Some may find this paper particularly hard to read not because its content is difficult but because it requires that the reader examine and question assumptions and premises that are most often taken completely for granted and hence not articulated at all. William James observed that there is no pain like the pain of a new idea. But this is only if the new idea is accepted and, by so doing, one has accepted the insecurity of realizing that one's model of reality has been inadequate or defective. A common refuge is to protect one's existing model of the world and to reject the new idea in rage. But economists, one likes to think, are more open-minded. In any case, many of the individual points made in the paper are not original. The originality mostly stems from putting together the various insights developed by others over the years. When these are assembled, the landscape looks considerably different — or to vary the metaphor, as in the poem about the six blind men and the elephant — each touching a different part had a different picture of the whole animal — when all the reports are in, what we have is a phenomenon of major importance.

I am acutely aware that this work is still very much work-in-progress. A great deal more could be done in further refining the arguments and in the presentation. Many more concrete examples could be advanced: every economist working on some set of real problems who has been exposed to this work has suggested a rich vein to be mined in his own field. From this point on, however, I believe that my marginal contribution will drop sharply and others can contribute more.

Except in a few cases, I have not presented examples for adverse criticism. In the unavoidable instances, what I have tried to pick are not the easy targets but the work of outstanding economists whose contributions otherwise are most deserving of admiration. In fact, at times a person whose work is cited has elsewhere, in a more reflective mood, demonstrated awareness of some of the same point that I am making. One drawback of this book, moreover, is that it may attract approval for the wrong reasons — that is, it may be misused in a general attack on the whole economic approach to policy-making. (Forty years ago, when being an economist was generally agreed to be sufficient to disqualify a person for membership on the Federal Reserve Board, this possibility would have been a weighty argument against writing this book.) What this work is meant to be is rather an attempt to strengthen economics as a means to understanding the economy and to improve its contribution to policy-making through a more realistic appreciation of what economics can really do.

The sympathetic reception to an initial presentation at Harvard from Edward S. Mason, whose guidance has been particularly valuable throughout my career, and from Arthur Smithies and Raymond Vernon encouraged me to go ahead. Thomas Mayer was generous in encouragement at a time when this was most needed. I have benefited from the comments of Irma Adelman, John M. Letiche and Theodore Morgan at seminars at Berkeley and Wisconsin and from Paul Streeten's and Gerald M. Meier's comments on an early draft. Guy Routh's and René Olivieri's perceptive suggestions were also most helpful for the final text. Although I encountered T. W. Hutchison's writings only late in this work, I was delighted to find support in them.

I am grateful to William Clark for making it possible for me to spend my last year with the World Bank working on this subject. Thanks are also due to Lester Gordon and Dwight H. Perkins, successive directors of the Harvard Institute of International Development, for making available the intellectual stimulation and facilities of Harvard University, and to my former colleagues at the World Bank, Benjamin B. King, Alexander Stevenson, Vincent Hogg, William Ward and Robert Youker for their helpful suggestions. Elizabeth K. Minnich and Pamela Dorn suggested some useful non-economic sources to me and Maria M. Collum patiently shepherded the manuscript through several revisions.

1

Introduction

. . .we must not look for the same degree of accuracy in all subjects; we must be content in each class of subjects with accuracy of such a kind as the subject-matter allows, and to such an extent as is proper to the inquiry.

Aristotle, *Nicomachean Ethics*

We have sought to justify our economic concepts in terms of considerations that are appropriate to the natural sciences; not observing that what economics tries to do . . . is essentially different.

John Hicks, *Wealth and Welfare*

The objectives of this book are to explore how closely economics relates to reality, and what this means for handling economic data, economic analysis and policy. In physics, quantum mechanics has demonstrated that there is an insuperable limit beyond which it is impossible in principle to know precisely both the exact position and the momentum of a simple elementary particle. In mathematics, Goedel proved that no axiomatic system could be complete. Economics is also subject to limitative results and the limits to precise knowledge of an economic situation or problem are approached rapidly. The mesh of the net that economists can weave to catch economic reality is much coarser than that of the natural scientists in their realm.

Central to the whole discussion are the meanings of the words 'accuracy' and 'precision'. In common usage, the meanings often overlap — there is a predisposition to believe that the more precise a statement is, the more accurate it is. For our purposes, it is necessary to make a clear distinction between them. 'Accuracy' will be used to convey the meaning of 'correctness', of 'true value'. 'Precision' will be used to convey the meaning of 'degree of sharpness' by which a thing or concept is specified. For example: on Cape Cod, where the pace of life is unhurried and casual, you may ask a craftsman in June when he will come to repair your fence. If he answers, 'Sometime in the autumn', he is being accurate but not precise. If he answers, 'Ten a.m., October 2', he is being precise but not accurate — it is almost certain that on October 2, the fish will be running and he will be out in his boat. One of the recurring themes that we will find in our discussion is that too often in economics the choice is between being roughly accurate or precisely wrong.

As is well known, Alfred Marshall and John Maynard Keynes, both of whom had had mathematical training, did not believe it was possible to apply exact mathematical methods to economics and, consequently, warned against them. Keynes endorsed Marshall's approach that a pervasive part of economic life cannot be precisely measured. As he stated in his famous footnote in his memorial of Alfred Marshall: economic interpretation in its highest form requires an '. . . amalgam of logic and intuition and the wide knowledge of facts, most of which are not precise. . .' (Keynes, 1925, p. 25).

To clear the ground, I would like first to state what this book is *not* about. It is *not* concerned with the question whether mathematics has any use in economics. I regard this as definitely settled — mathematics is useful as an economic language, as an efficient technique of reasoning and logic, as an essential part of the logico-mathematical framework of economic theory; in short, mathematics is an indispensable tool in economics. (I do not believe, however, that the use of mathematics in economics is justified by the argument that we need the shelter of Mathematics to protect Economics from intruders (Dasgupta, 1968, p. 4).) Mathematics is not, however, a perfect substitute for language — not every communication among human beings can be expressed as well by mathematics as by words. The meaning of a mathematical symbol does not change, once defined, whereas words can flirt with meanings and coquette with relationships. Words can be deliberately ambiguous where relationships are ambiguous and it is desired to leave them so; many a peace treaty if written in maths would never have been signed. One could argue that the whole of constitutional law in countries with written constitutions is essentially involved in the changing meaning of words in new circumstances and new times. Poetry can never be perfectly translated even from one language into another and certainly not into mathematics. In sum, natural language can be more flexible in conveying meaning, it is infinitely richer in vocabulary than mathematics, and frequently it can be more accurate although less precise.

What this book *is* concerned with is the application of theory to economic reality: is the result meaningful when mathematical symbols or words are replaced by numbers that are intended accurately to explain or to forecast the real world? Certainly, one can conceive that every detail of human economic behaviour could be expressed mathematically, but this does not mean that the mathematical expression in question actually can be produced within the body of mathematical theory that now exists or that may ever exist (Arrow, 1951, p. 130). Moreover, it does not follow at all that because mathematics may allow us to describe the general outlines of a system of relationship as algebraic equations we can then always discover the specific numbers to replace the symbols to make the equations fit the particular situation we are concerned with. Hayek has pointed out that the founders of modern mathematical economics had no such illusions. For example, Pareto clearly stated it would be absurd to assume we could ascertain all the data needed for his system of equations describing market equilibrium that would make it possible to calculate the prices and quantities of the commodities and services sold (Hayek, 1975, p. 35).

The discussion in this book is based on the assumption — often falsified in reality — that the mathematics used in economics is not mishandled. Paul Streeten has called attention to the danger that use of mathematics may create a false sense of certainty: there is a temptation to mistake 'validity' for 'truth'. That is, the correct deduction of logical conclusions is mistaken for the discovery of facts about the real world. Another temptation is sub-optimization; that is, to assume that only what is quantifiable is important and to forget the rest. 'The result may be the worst of all possible worlds. . . . rationality about a sub-system can be worse than sub-rationality about the whole system' (Streeten, 1972, p. 371).

Underlying much of the practice of modern economists is a silent premise that the formal properties of the mathematical symbols used in economic models must be isomorphous with the empirical relations they purport to represent in the real world; that is, that the two complex structures — the model and the reality to which it refers — can be mapped onto each other in such a way that to each significant part of one structure there is a corresponding part of the other structure and each of these has the same functional role in their respective structures. A good example of isomorphism is the relationship between the notes shown on a musical score and the sounds of the composition when it is perfectly played. (For economists, perhaps, the best example is the isomorphism between the curves in a Cartesian plane and the corresponding equations in two variables — in mapping from one onto the other all the relevant information is preserved.)

This assumption can be accepted in physics, for example, because of the very way in which physical models are defined and developed. In physics *only* the quantities that can be represented numerically and transformed mathematically are permitted. In fact, physics defines itself as. . .'the science devoted to discovering, developing and refining those aspects of reality that are amenable to mathematical analysis' (Zinman, 1978, p. 28). In economics, isomorphism cannot be tacitly accepted; the relationship between models and reality is a central problem to be examined in each case. This book is largely involved with this theme.

There is an astounding proposition in economics advanced by Milton Friedman and accepted by many economists that what matters in an economic hypothesis is only successful prediction. Further, Friedman argues that not only does it not matter whether the assumptions are unrealistic but even, paradoxically, 'to be important . . . a hypothesis must be descriptively *false* in its assumptions . . .' (1953, p. 15; my emphasis). (Friedman's argument may depend in part on confusing abstraction — i.e., identifying or separating relevant factors from a cloud of irrelevant detail — with the difference between falsehood and truth. That is, since abstraction does not reproduce 'noise' but only 'signal', it must be 'false'.) His discussion demonstrates that he really believes that it is irrelevant whether the assumptions of a theory are a false representation of reality or not. As long as the predictions of a theory appear to be accurate that is all that matters to him.

A most important application of Friedman's approach is his belief that it does not really matter whether it is true or not that all consumers maximize their utility and all businesses maximize their profits, since the economic system functions in such a way that the results come out just *as if* they did try to maximize. Consequently, we do not need to worry what the facts are of behaviour or of motivation in the real world. The basic fallacy here is that nobody knows whether the firms that have survived are truly profit-maximizers or not (Blaug, 1980, pp. 116 – 19). In an industry with increasing returns to scale the existing firms may simply be the ones that entered first and a late-entry profit-maximizer may never have been able to catch up; or the survivors may simply be the ones that had an advantageous power position such as special relationship to a bank or to a government agency, etc. One cannot assume that what exists is the maximizing best of all possible worlds.

Friedman's simple prediction criterion eliminates one of the most important functions of a scientific theory — that is, to provide an understanding of the events and processes that underlie the predicted results. In natural science, it is not sufficient to predict the position of a pointer on a dial, the theory must also explain why the pointer takes up that particular position and only that position. Discovering a correlation is not the same as discovering a causal relationship. Since antiquity the relationship between the moon and the tides has been known, but there was no adequate theory of the tides until Newton's theory of gravitation explained why the tides and their heights occurred just when and how they did. Only when we have adequate theories that explain how the economy works in addition to predicting outcomes can we begin to consider economic policies that can effectively control or change the economy.

The second drawback to Friedman's position is that even if a theory has appeared to provide successful predictions in the past on the basis of false or unrealistic assumptions, one can have no confidence that it will continue to provide successful predictions. It is easy with the help of a calculator and some idle time to come up with obviously nonsensical theories that appear to show a record of successful predictions. For example, David F. Hendry, with tongue in cheek, has demonstrated that cumulative rainfall predicts the rate of inflation in the United Kingdom (Hendry, 1980, pp. 391 – 5). Then there is the Boston Snow Theory: if there is snow on the ground in Boston on Christmas Day, that indicates the following year will be good for the American economy. This is all pseudo-science. In science, merely discovering a series of coincidences linking premises and conclusions does not demonstrate a correct theory. An acceptable theory must have assumptions isomorphic to reality, a clear chain of correct logical or logico-mathematical reasoning leading to conclusions that can be tested for isomorphism to reality; if a single link is broken, the theory fails. If assumptions inconsistent with reality appear to lead to true conclusions, then the chain of logic is wrong, the result is a coincidence, or the conclusions are suspect.

At the purely mathematical stage, an economic model or 'pure' theory can be like a story in science fiction or a game whose rules we make up ourselves. At this stage, our main criteria are only that the rules be logically consistent and the system complete (i.e. internally consistent), whether or not it corresponds in any respect to the real world. While our bodies must function in the real economy, constrained by the limitations and natural laws of reality, our imagination is free to soar above it. But when we must cope with the real economy and our model is needed to solve a real problem, to explain, predict or change reality, then the model must be externally consistent (isomorphic) with the real world: one can no longer assume that we can travel at speeds greater than the speed of light or that our concepts grasp reality more precisely or that our parameters can be measured more accurately than the real world permits (Weizenbaum, 1976, pp. 43 – 4). Econometric models that assume accuracy and precision beyond the margins set by reality have no practical usefulness (other than as games, teaching aids or as kinds of finger exercises) and bear the same relationship to economics and economic policy as scientific fiction has to science — that is, they may require a good deal of imagination and pseudo-scientific calculation but are of no help in coping with the real world.

Perhaps the greatest difficulty economists face in the transition from the ivory-tower of theory to coping with the problems of decision-making in the real economic world is in shifting from the precise numbers and well-behaved models of pure theory to the rough inaccurate data, recalcitrant behaviour and shifting complexities of reality. The transition is particularly difficult because there is little or nothing in economists' training to prepare them for this stark contrast. On the contrary, the conscious or unconscious concept that many economists have of economics as a science comparable to physics leads them to expect that they should be able to explain economic reality with the same precision and predictability that mechanics in physics has been able to attain in explaining and predicting phenomena in the universe. (Georgescu-Roegen's definitive destruction of the mechanics model for economics, 1974, has not yet penetrated much of the profession. See also Hutchison, 1977, Ch. III; Lowe, 1965, pp. 34 – 61; and Sidney Schoeffler's neglected contribution, 1955.)

Even more, there is an unconscious tendency among economists to believe that mathematical rigour *requires* absolute precision in the numbers used. This is not so. John von Neumann, perhaps the greatest mathematician of our time, has specifically dealt with this. He has pointed out that, while in all mathematical problems the answer is required with absolute rigor and absolute reliability, this need not mean that it is also required with absolute precision. In most problems in applied mathematics and mathematical physics the precision that is wanted is quite limited. The data are often not known to better than a few (say 5) per cent, and the result may be satisfactory to even less precision (say 10 per cent). This is compatible with absolute mathematical rigour if the sensitivity of the result to changes in the data as well as the amount of precision of the result are rigorously known (von Neumann, 1963, pp. 324 – 5).

The objective of this book is not only to show that precision in economics is limited but also to attempt to offer a more realistic operational expectation. Quantification and the use of mathematics and statistics in economics are indispensable but it is also essential to recognize clearly that economic reality can be accurately circumscribed only within differing margins of precision. This book is concerned, therefore, with that uneasy frontier-zone where economic theory meets the real world of human beings and institutions. It is concerned with how good a grasp economics can get of that hazy, elusive and changing sector of human life called the economy.

2

Problems of Measurement in General

> When a problem in pure or in applied mathematics is 'solved' by numerical computation, errors, that is, deviations of the numerical 'solution' obtained from the true, rigorous one, are unavoidable. Such a 'solution' is therefore meaningless, unless there is an estimate of the total error in the above sense.
>
> John von Neumann, *Collected Works*, vol. V

Although modern economics has prided itself on its apparent similarity to physics, one of the very first basic lessons taught in beginning physics — that it is essential to understand, to evaluate and to express the degree of accuracy represented by each number used — is generally ignored and neglected in economics. Modern economists insist on quantification but completely overlook the need to understand how much precision is actually attainable in the accuracy of the numbers used as well as the need to express the margin of error present in an economic measurement. Sampling errors for an indifferent (i.e. not hostile) universe are estimated and are usually stated, but the limits of accuracy in most economic estimates that are very rough are usually not stated and sometimes not even acknowledged. Furthermore, economists are not trained to handle this set of problems. Instead, even though quite aware that their data (GNP estimates, costs, prices, rates of return), produced for them by others, are not fully reliable, economists operate with these numbers as though they were precisely accurate to the first or second decimal point.

Norbert Wiener, the noted scientist, observed in this regard that social scientists did not appear to understand the intellectual attitude that underlay the success of mathematical physics. The frequent practice in economics of developing an elaborate model with a relative or total indifference to the methods and possibilities of observing or measuring the elusive quantities concerned is exactly counter to the real spirit of the hard sciences. A true science has to begin with a critical understanding of its quantifiable elements and the means adopted for measuring them (Wiener, 1964, pp. 89 – 90).

A generation later, Wiener's comment appears still to be fully applicable. Thomas Mayer (1980) has spelled out how econometricians continue to violate the basic requirements of real scientific procedure. For example, it is likely that most econometricians still do not even bother to check that their data are properly copied from their sources through the preparation for the computer to the final printout. Very little attention is paid to the quality of data — data are dumped into a computer without close examination. Students are not taught to keep, nor do practitioners maintain, adequate research records. More prestige is acquired from applying the latest complex techniques to good, bad or indifferent data than in arriving at valid, verifiable and useful results. As a consequence of all this, there is apparently frequent non-replicability of results. Very few attempts are made and published of checks of previous findings of econometric research.

Even if unscientific statistical and econometric methods are avoided, errors in economic data will still exist: errors in economic data *are inherent* and unavoidable. Why is this so? First of all, errors are inevitable whenever the transition is made from a purely mathematical model using only symbols to a numerical or econometric model. This is true not only of economic models but of all models. John von Neumann and H. H. Goldstine in their pioneering study (1963) identified four primary sources of errors in all numerical computations. To the extent that an economic decision involves the use of numbers, these sources of errors are therefore also present and need to be taken into account.

First, in applied mathematics the model chosen to represent the underlying problem will represent it only with certain abstractions and simplifications. A mathematical formulation necessarily represents only a more or less explicit theory of some phase of reality; it is not reality itself (von Neumann and Goldstine, 1963, p. 428). In economics, this first step of abstraction from reality may be even greater than that identified by von Neumann and Goldstine — and the resulting inherent errors consequently are greater. In the social sciences it is very easy to formulate a theoretical model where the determination of the optimum statistical model entails mathematical problems that no one yet has been able to solve. There are also models where the problems are soluble in principle by known methods but the computations in practice would take an impossibly long time. In these cases, the procedure is to substitute a mathematically practicable theory, as similar as possible to the desired one (Arrow, 1951, p. 132). In other words, the model used is at second remove from reality — it is a proxy for the unrealizable ideal model, which itself would be an abstraction from reality.

Second, the model may involve parameters, the values of which have to be derived directly or indirectly from observations. These parameters are affected by errors, and these errors cause errors in the results (von Neumann and Goldstine, 1963, p. 482). This comment is deceptively simple: errors in parameters derive not only from the process of measurement of sharply defined individuals or classes but also from the definition of the individuals and classes being measured. As we shall see in the next chapter, the causes of errors in observations are much more prevalent and stronger in economics than in the physical sciences.

Third, the model will in general involve transcendental operations (like integration or differentiation) and implicit definitions (such as solutions of algebraical or transcendental equations). 'In order to be approached by numerical calculation, these have to be replaced by elementary processes (involving only those elementary arithmetical operations which the computer can handle directly) and explicit definitions which correspond to a finite, constructive procedure that resolves itself into a linear sequence of steps.' All these processes are approximative, and so the *strict* mathematical statement we start with is now replaced by 'an *approximate* one' (pp. 482 – 3; emphasis in original).

The fourth source of errors comes from the need to round off numbers. There has to be a cut-off somewhere, that is, a maximum number of places in a number. From this point on these 'noise variables or round off variables' are injected into the computation every time an elementary operation is performed and constitute a source of errors (pp. 484 – 5).

In modern computers there are usually two distinct ways of handling numerical data. In Fortran, for example, numerical data are either in integer numbers or 'floating-point numbers'. Integer numbers are the numbers we customarily use. Floating-point numbers use scientific notation, that is, a number is expressed as a base number (mantissa) times 10 raised to some power (exponent). Instead of writing a number as, say, 430, it could be written as 43×10 or 4.3×10^2 or 0.43×10^3 with the decimal point thus 'floating' as desired. In this way, a number is stored in the computer as a sign bit, a string of bits representing the exponent and a string representing the mantissa. Because the range of floating-point numbers is much greater than that of integers for the same number of bits, most computations work with floating-point mantissa. Floating-point numbers tend to lose accuracy in the course of calculations when the product of two numbers, for example, results in a mantissa with more significant bits than can be retained for storage. In adding numbers, all must have the same exponent, which means shifting the points in any mantissas accordingly, and again some bits of information may have to be eliminated.

These four sources of error are inherent in any numerical model whether in the natural sciences or in economics. Economics has additional problems. Natural scientists learn at the very beginning of their training to be aware of the inevitability of errors and how to deal with them. One of the techniques they learn is 'significant digits', which teaches an appreciation of the degree of accurate precision that a number represents and, consequently, how to avoid meaningless manipulation of 'noise'. Briefly, this technique shows that the degree of precise accuracy in the final outcome of an arithmetical operation is determined by the most imprecise number involved in the operation (see Technical Appendix). Not only are economists not trained how best to cope with errors but economics has much greater problems in this regard than most of the natural sciences. In the next chapter, we shall concentrate on the special factors that make accuracy in the observation and calculation of economic parameters and variables more difficult than similar operations in the physical sciences.

3

Special Sources of Inaccuracy in Economic Data

> . . .the difference between facts which are what they are independent of human desire and endeavor and facts which are to some extent what they are because of human interest and purpose, and which alter with alteration in the latter, cannot be got rid of by any methodology. The more sincerely we appeal to facts, the greater is the importance of the distinction between facts which condition human activity and facts which are conditioned by human activity. In the degree which we ignore this difference, social science becomes pseudoscience.
>
> John Dewey, *The Public and its Problems*

The preceding chapter called attention to the fact that in all sciences — natural or social — in all attempts to apply theoretical models to reality a margin of error is inevitably introduced as numbers are involved. In economics, there are several additional important sources of errors. The first comes in the gathering and the processing of economic data. The second comes in extending economic analysis from individual to group behaviour. Then there is the central role that prediction of the future plays in economic decision-making and the impact of the unavoidable uncertainty of the future on the economic data that are involved. Although we must deal with the important problem of the relation of economic data to the economic concepts that the data are supposed to measure, in this chapter we take as an assumption that A that is being measured can be precisely defined and separated from non-A by a sharp boundary.

Inaccuracy in economic observations

'Accuracy' refers to whether a number correctly represents the 'true value' of a particular measurement or observation. 'True values' are numbers that measure a particular class of homogeneous objects in a unique procedure that yields unique results. The ordered pair (a_0, n_0) is unique: the object a_0 that is being measured relates to the number n_0 in accordance with a specified rule; there is a one-to-one correspondence between them (Koerner, 1966, pp. 148 – 50). In economics, counting the amount of cash held by an individual at a particular instant in time is an example: assuming no desire to misrepresent and no clerical or mechanical errors, the true value can be ascertained accurately and precisely to the last penny.

The analysis of inaccuracy in economic observations was well covered in Oskar Morgenstern's devastating but neglected classic, *On the Accuracy of Economic Observations* (1963). (It is significant that even in his Festschrift — *Essays in Mathematical Economics in Honor of Oskar Morgenstern*, edited by Martin Shubik — not one of the 30 essays contributed was concerned with the ideas in this book.) Morgenstern emphasized several innate sources of errors in economic observations: economic data are not usually secured from planned experiments but rather are the by-products or results of business and government activities; they are usually gathered not by highly trained economist observers but by clerical personnel or people employed ad hoc; the data collected are often defined by legal rather than economic categories; consequently, the data frequently describe or measure a category that is somewhat different from what the economist would want — that is, what is available is a more or less imperfect proxy for the parameter or variable that is really needed.

The sorts of errors that creep into economic statistics as a result are illustrated by a study by Ernest Rudd on data on British industry (1954 – 55). The published statistics derive from primary data collected within the firm. One of the most common initial sources is the 'little black book' of the foreman in charge of a job — and often the foreman is only semi-literate. One investigator into the efficiency of horse transport discovered data showing remarkable performance by horses at one depot. In fact, the depot had no horses at all and was reporting on motor trucks on the wrong form. Often the data reported come from reports set up by the firm for its own use; these may be based on certain conventions useful to the firm, which may not be explained when the data are supplied. Sometimes, the employee keeping the records has his own conventions; when he changes jobs there is probably a change in the methods by which the records are kept. RAF clerks sending in reports on mechanical trouble with different aircraft used to omit the most common type of fault because 'everyone' knew that the X-type aeroplanes had that sort of trouble! Then, there are all the human misunderstandings and biases that get involved in all human endeavours: successes are more fully disclosed than failures, data that support a position are more available than the opposite, etc.

Rudd's conclusions were that this does not mean that most of the data used in economics are completely unreliable but it does mean that there is a large margin of measurement error that is much larger than the 'relatively unimportant sampling errors' that are usually allowed for. And, finally, that: 'Any change which is to be measured with reasonable certainty has to be of fair size' (1954 – 55, p. 76).

There is also a complex set of problems stemming from the unavoidable imprecision of accounting. Accountants freely admit that theirs is an imprecise art but economists often do not appreciate how much judgement does enter into producing corporate accounts. For example, a company may decide to switch from FIFO to LIFO for inventory accounting. Under FIFO (first in, first out), when a widget is shipped out the company takes as its cost what it paid for the oldest widget on its shelves. When prices are going up this makes profits look good. Under LIFO (last in, last out), the cost is taken as being the price paid by the company for the last widget bought on the shelves. This makes profits lower but more accurate. But making the profit statement more realistic makes the balance sheet less accurate. Usually when a company changes from FIFO to LIFO, its existing stock of raw materials, goods in process and finished commodities stays on the accounts at the old costs, which during an inflation constantly lag behind current costs. If a company cuts production below sales and reduces its inventory, its profits are misleadingly higher while it is selling off older lower-costed goods (Greene, 1982 p. 171).

The possible warping of data by their sources is usually overlooked in econometric work. As explained by Carl F. Christ, the econometric work of the Cowles Commission, for example, assumed that, except for definitions, no numerical theory (i.e. an equation) fits the relevant facts exactly. Many equations fit the relevant facts approximately, with errors or deviations that are sometimes positive and sometimes negative. Accordingly, these are added on explicitly into each equation as an extra term, the value of which changes with each observation so that the equation always remains exactly true. The assumption is that the values of the deviations in any equation are determined as if by chance or at random. The major factors involved in a particular economic relationship are presumably accounted for explicitly by separate variables. The remaining minor factors are thrown into the random term, and the net effect of a large number of small unrelated causes almost always acts as if it were really random (Christ, 1952, pp. 32 – 3).

Morgenstern's point is completely overlooked in this approach: in the real world the whole perception of economic reality — grasped in a particular equation, numerical parameters, variables and error term — may be warped by the economic interests of the observed in providing the data the equation is based on. The underlying, but unexpressed, assumption in the Cowles Commission work was that the only errors that need to be taken into account are those that keep the 'relevant facts' from fitting neatly into an equation. The *real* problem may be that the 'relevant facts' are only known inaccurately and what is reported may have been deliberately warped, if not completely falsified.

In brief, gathering economic statistics is a two-person game. In an atomistic market, there is little incentive to hold back, conceal or distort information on the part of any one of the participants. In sectors dominated by large corporations, the situation may be very different. James T. Bonnen, in his presidential address to the American Agricultural Economics Association, pointed out that increasingly in the food and fibre sector, for example, essential information is held by a few firms whose immediate interests are often not served by releasing that information (Bonnen, 1975, p. 756). No electron profits from deceiving a physicist, but the sources of economic statistics may have a direct interest in reporting inaccurately or falsifying economic data (e.g. business and individual tax returns; government defence, aid and intelligence expenditures). Shackle makes this point even more graphically: human forces in a world of rivalry and struggle are partly *directed* to the creation of a 'fog of ignorance and confusion' (1955, p. 38).

A striking example of this point is the spread of the so-called 'subterranean' or 'underground' economy. The deliberate conceal-ment of large numbers of economic transactions from official government notice has been well known for centuries in countries like Italy, France and Spain where tax evasion is a universal fact. In recent years, it has become evident that the 'underground economy' has become an important factor in India and in most other less developed countries, in the Eastern European countries, in the United States and in the United Kingdom, and is not unknown in the Scandinavian countries. In market economies, the incentive for tax evasion becomes increasingly stronger as inflation moves people's incomes up into higher tax brackets. In India, it is irresistible: at the higher income levels, if a businessman honestly declared his income, after paying income tax, wealth tax and a 'compulsory deposit', he would actually finish with a negative net income (*Economist*, 1980c).

A similar distorting force may stem from political factors. That is, the character of a political system may substantially influence the degree of accuracy of economic data. The closeness of the ap-proach of economic data to accurately reflecting reality may depend on how open and pluralistic the distribution of political power is in a system. The more political power is concentrated and removed from control by the people, the more inaccurate the statistical data are likely to be. The official organ of the Central Committee of the Chinese Communist Party, the Peking *People's Daily*, has admitted that, up to as late as 1979, it simply invented information to portray life in China in a rosier light (Reich-Ranicki, 1980, p. 62). In some sophisticated cases, distortion is ac-complished through suppression of key statistics. In all countries, the budgets of intelligence agencies are concealed in the budgets of other departments.

Uncertainty of the future

While there may be a great deal of aesthetic pleasure in economic theory, economic history or economic analysis for their own sakes, the most important reason for the existence of these and other branches of economics is their guidance in the making of economic decisions. But economic decisions depend on predictions of future economic data. How accurate can such predictions be?

Kenneth Arrow has shown that uncertainties in predicting future prices, quantities, technologies and tastes are so great that an adequate set of markets for future goods cannot exist. That is, whereas a flour miller can protect himself by buying today in the grain futures market wheat to be delivered, say, 90 days from now, there is not and cannot be such a possibility of buying and selling future goods and services for most commodities and services of interest to most of us (Arrow, 1974a). Yet individuals and enterprises must make decisions every day on the basis of some sort of prediction in all of these cases.

Before one can predict the future, it is necessary to know the present. However, there is an unavoidable lag of statistics behind events. In a few cases, this lag is very small — stock prices are reported almost instantaneously — but usually it will take days, weeks or months before statistics can be collected and compiled to inform the economic analyst of what has been happening. Because of the different lags, there is a constant need to revise the estimates that have been prepared. This means that before one can make decisions or forecasts about the future, it is necessary first, as Cairncross aptly put it, 'to forecast the present'. The result is that one may be making decisions about the future when one's knowledge of the present or immediate past is really incorrect.

In 1976, the British Treasury estimated that the United Kingdom's GNP was growing by only 1½ per cent and the balance of trade deficit was around $3 billion. As a result, the pound dropped from $2.20 to $1.58 and the aid of the International Monetary Fund was called for. The subsequent revised statistics revealed there had been no real crisis: 1976 GNP growth was most satisfactory at nearly 4 per cent and the balance of trade deficit was less than half the original estimate (*Forbes*, 1980, p. 144). In early 1981, the British national accounts showed that, in the last quarter of 1980, GDP was recovering from a slump, or had levelled off, or was still falling — depending on whether one looked at income data, expenditure data or output data.

A large part of the impulse behind the supply-side economics that dominated President Reagan's early administration and led to the sweeping tax cuts of 1981 was based on the belief that the investment rate in American industry has declined and new tax incentives were, therefore, needed. In fact, later revised GNP estimates show instead that the ratio of US fixed non-residential investment to GNP had *increased* by 2 percentage points during 1977 – 81 compared to 1960 – 64 (11.3 per cent compared to 9.3 per cent).

Forecasting future parameters or variables is incomparably more difficult in economics than in the physical sciences. In physics, for example, there are essentially a limited number of important factors involved in any problem and their role either does not change over time or changes in a regular predictable way. The parameters are constant and it has proved possible in many cases to ascertain quite precisely what these constants are. In astronomy, it has been possible to build on hundreds of years of observations of what are mainly constant or stable phenomena.

In fields concerned with human behaviour like economics, in contrast, constant or stable phenomena can rarely be relied on. Projections of population size, for example, are immeasurably simpler than most economic projections since they are concerned with large numbers and a few natural biological parameters, yet they have almost notoriously proved unreliable. The UK Central Policy Review Staff, reviewing the British population projections made from 1955 to 1974, found that the size of population forecast for the year 2000 has varied between 50 million and 70 million and the projected number of annual live births has varied between 650,000 and 1,500,000. In brief, aside from mortality, the other two factors affecting population — fertility and immigration — have proved impossible to predict over the long term (*Economist*, 1977, p. 4). Even figures on the size of today's population have large margins of error.

These points on population projections are illuminating and alarming enough, yet forecasts of economic data are usually considerably more difficult to compute. In forecasting money supply figures, the errors frequently blanket the area in which most of the controversy over policy takes place. A governor of the US central bank found that the errors in projecting changes in the rate of growth of money supply were close to 50 per cent (Maisel, 1973, p. 186). With the growth of the US budget it has become evident that the US government cannot forecast its own expenditures accurately, much less its revenues. Between January and July 1978, for example, the Office of Management and Budget (OMB) lowered its estimates of 1978 spending by $11 billion or 2 per cent of the total (Penner, 1978, p. 2).

The subject matter of economics does not possess the constancies and absence of significant historical change and development of physics. Not only do the structural relationships change over time, often unpredictably and irregularly, but the economy is buffeted by unpredictable, often arbitrary and irrational political changes at home and abroad (e.g. OPEC in 1973 and 1979). The factors involved in the structural relationships often reach outside the economy and use their influence in the political sphere to get the economic parameters changed for their own benefit.

Endogenous factors, too, produce unpredictability in economic systems. The units under observation (individual human beings, groups or organizations) for whose behaviour a prediction is to be made are themselves also making their own analyses and decisions based on their own predictions of the future. A scientist observing a planet and predicting its future orbit does not have to cope with the planet itself making *its own* appreciation of the situation and changing its present orbit depending upon its prediction of the future (see Lowe, 1965, p. 97).

The 'Rational Expectations' school of economists is, therefore, right in arguing that it is essential to adopt the realistic assumption that in making policy the government must realize that economic agents like consumers or investors, for instance, will not carry on mechanically no matter what the government does. Instead, they will adjust their behaviour according to their rational expectations of how the economy is likely to be affected — and in the process they may frustrate what the government had hoped to achieve. This is much more sensible than the assumption underlying most macro-models that past structural relationships will persist in the future with only slow adaptive changes to major policy decisions. However, the school then goes on to adopt unrealistic assumptions of its own: that individuals always use available information efficiently and understand the structure of the economy and so can clearly foresee the results of policy changes, and that the economy is in continuous equilibrium. Finally, some of the models the school constructs fall into the same fixed relationships trap as the models it criticizes — they make expectations of prices, for example, an objective endogenous variable based on past changes in prices coupled with a correction for past forecasting errors. While it is true in some situations that people's expectations of the future solely depend on their experience of the past, in other cases, with a major new development (OPEC, for example), people may be forced to reorganize their perceptions and expect something that never happened to them before (see Willes, 1981, p. 91, and Hahn, 1981, p. 133).

In this connection, Georgescu-Roegen argues that Pareto was wrong in believing that it is only the impossibility of the immensity of the number of equations to be solved that keeps economics from being a numerical science on a par with astronomy (1971, p. 335). The really insuperable obstacle is that human beings cannot accurately forecast their own reactions: once an economic situation changes, *ex post* an individual may discover that what he had thought were his preferences have in fact altered. No process in which the Oedipus effect is at work can be represented by an analytical model: the announcement of an action to be taken changes the evidence upon which each individual bases his expectations and causes him to revise his previous plans. Further, if you decide to make your decision about whether or not you will purchase a car only when the spring comes, not before, it is impossible for you or anyone else to predict what you will do.

The difficulty of formulating an objective criterion for decisions involving uncertainty stems directly from the fact that corresponding expectations may not be ordinally measurable, probably not even comparable, and have only a distant and debatable connection with past observations. Only in games can one rely on being able to evaluate accurately in precise numbers the objective probability of an expectation. In the real economic world this can rarely happen. If a piece of land can be used only for building a luxury hotel, its evaluation may depend on the economic development of the country, the future course of foreign exchange rates, whether an airport is built or upgraded, etc. — all judgements about uncertain expectations that cannot be accurately precise numerically (Menger, 1967, p. 230).

This difficulty of assigning a precisely accurate number to each expectation is qualitatively different from the difficulty inherent in accurate measurement in all sciences. In the physical sciences, in measuring 'M', the difficulty is that of precisely locating its partner number from an ordinally measurable scale. In economics, we do not have the ordinally measurable set of which the expectation is an element (Georgescu-Roegen, 1958, p. 27).

The future presents us with a spectrum of uncertainty. Some of this relates to risks whose objective probability distributions are more or less precisely and accurately known from past experience of a large number of random events (e.g. house fires that can be insured against). Some of the spectrum consists of risks where relatively firm subjective probabilities can be estimated (e.g. a successful entrepreneur making rational judgements on the quantitative probability of success of a new initiative in his field). The rest of the spectrum increasingly involves risks where the estimates of probabilities deteriorate from cases where some semblance of ordering is possible (e.g. doing this is likely to be more dangerous than that) to those where there is just no evidence presently available on which a judgement can be made. At this end of the spectrum we cannot evade uncertainty by assuming that the world is statistically predictable, that we possess actuarial knowledge about future costs and benefits and, therefore, that the future can be represented by known probability distributions that make it possible for us to act as if we possessed absolute foreknowledge (Davidson, 1981, p. 161; for a more comprehensive presentation, see Hicks, 1979, ch. 8).

Economists have been led astray by the mechanics analogy. Subconsciously, many economists tend to feel that our predicted data, like those of astronomers predicting an eclipse, should be precise, unequivocal and unconditional. But this standard is inherently impossible in economics. This does not mean, however, that we need to abandon all prediction. We have uncertainty as to the *precise* shape of the future but this does not mean that nothing can be known. There are large areas of relative stability is economic life and the amount of possible change has a time dimension. We cannot rely on precise laws in economics. Paul Samuelson has written that he has learned how treacherous 'economic laws' are (e.g. Pareto's Law of unchangeable inequality of incomes; Colin Clark's Law of a 25 per cent ceiling on government expenditure and taxation; Marx's Law of the falling rate of real wage; Everybody's Law of a constant capital – output ratio) (Samuelson, 1964, p. 336). However, we can ascertain particular patterns of economic behaviour in quantifiable form for particular times and particular economies. From these we can ascertain tendencies and trends that provide a basis for predictions. Such predictions can never be as precisely accurate in their time dimensions or in their results as predictions in the physical sciences because a 'trend' is not a law — it can change tomorrow. This means that, unlike the physicists or astronomers, our predictions need to include the consideration of possible changes in our parameters as well as in our variables.

If we have to have a natural science analogy, meteorology is a more appropriate one for us. Meteorology too has to cope with a system in constant flux, a near to infinite set of endogenous and exogenous factors, and the variability of probable outcomes grows exponentially with time. At the World Climate Conference in February 1979, the world's leading students of climate concluded that we can say with some confidence that the amount of carbon dioxide in the atmosphere has increased by about 15 per cent during the last century. However, it is not certain whether this will result in the climate's getting warmer or colder! It was agreed that there has been a cooling trend in the northern hemisphere for the last few decades but whether it will continue or not is unknown. Compared to the record of meteorology in predicting weather and climatic change, the accomplishments of economics are not unfavourable.

4

Loose Concepts and Economics

Etsi autem empirice non posset haberi perfecta aestimatio, non ideo
minus empirica aestimatio in praxis utilis et sufficiens foret. (Yet
although empirical calculation cannot be exact, it may be sufficient
and useful in practice.)

Leibnitz, letter to Bernouilli, 3 December, 1703

Der Mangel an mathematischer Bildung gibt sich durch nichts so
auffallend zu erkennen, wie durch masslose Schaerfe im
Zahlenrechnen. (The lack of mathematical learning reveals itself in
nothing so strikingly as in unlimited precision in numerical
computations.)

C. F. W. Gauss (quoted in Oskar Morgenstern, *On the Accuracy of
Economic Observations*; my translation)

In the last chapter we were concerned with accuracy, that is,
whether a number correctly represents the 'true value', past, present or future. This, of course, assumes that a 'true value' really
exists that we are trying to observe or measure. In the physical
sciences, it is accepted that repeated measurements of a particular
parameter, say the length of a piece of wood, will approach the true
length insofar as this ideal 'true value' can be revealed through
measurement. Budding scientists learn that the repeated measurement readings will usually differ from each other because the rule
is not perfect, the angle of the eye has changed, etc. The readings
will, however, tend to cluster around a central average. The more
measurements that are made, the more the readings will cluster and
the more likely it is that this central average represents the 'true
value' of the length. Since perfectly exact measurement of most

quantities is not possible, what scientists work with are figures that are the outcome of this process of repeated measurement. Consequently, careful scientific practice is to state the results of measurements with margins of error, i.e. a given piece of wood is 8 ± 0.05 cm long (E. Adams, 1965; Koerner, 1966; Margenau, 1959). In economic life, as we have seen, the reports of economic data may be deliberately biased because of the intervention of human motives and the results, therefore, may fall outside the spread of measurements caused by the state of nature or instrumental uncertainties.

There is an even more important reason for failure to grasp reality with precise accuracy by economic concepts. This gap between economic theory and empirical reality stems from the very nature of economic reality itself. Stephan Koerner (1966) has analyzed the relationship between theory and reality most ably and in the following brief exposition I shall make use of his analysis.

In a scientific theoretical system with a logical – mathematical framework such as economics, the basic unit is the 'individual'. The 'individual' may be, for example, a consumer or a commodity like an automobile. An individual is an entity that either is indivisible into parts or loses its individuality when it is divided and the parts are separated from each other. *In theory*, the individual is definite and unchangeable — sharply distinguished from its background and sharply demarcated from other individuals and in time. *In reality*, even though usually we may have no doubt whether a particular entity is an 'individual' or not, doubt may enter as soon as a time or space dimension comes into play. Indefiniteness in some phase or respect of an individual is completely compatible with definiteness otherwise. In the case of a human individual, for instance, the whole controversy over abortion is a disagreement over *exactly when* the entity (zygote, embryo or foetus) destined to acquire the attributes of a human being should be considered to be a 'human being'. At present (1983), the legal system has not yet definitively agreed at what point in the loss of bodily functions a dying person should be considered dead. When does a motor car begin or cease to exist? How much exactly of its parts can we take away from a car without destroying the individual car? As we shall see, the lack of definiteness of the individual, either in space or in time, is important in much of economics.

Second, *in theory*, classes and the concepts relating to them are exact: A either possesses the predicate that makes it a member of class p or it does not. That is, A must be either a member of P or a member of non-P. There are no neutral candidates. One cannot say A_n is a borderline case, being just barely a member of P and of non-P. This violates one of the main principles of logic — something cannot be both P and non-P. Similarly, one cannot say that A_n is just barely not a member of P and also just not a member of P. This violates another logical principle — a thing must be either a member of P or it must be non-P. However, once we return to reality, neutral or borderline candidates are common to most of the classes we deal with.

In economic reality, the classes we deal with are usually inexact. For example, is the purchase of a house an investment or a consumption item? It can be either or both. Purchases and mortgage costs of new houses are included in the consumer price index, yet some people buy houses they will live in partly or wholly as an investment in the hope of getting capital gains. In the United States, until the Supreme Court ruled otherwise in 1981, when an employer provided meals or lodging to workers for his convenience (e.g. workers fed and housed on an offshore drilling rig to keep them on hand in case of need), such benefits were 'wages' on which social security and unemployment taxes were to be paid but they were not 'wages' in calculating income tax liability.

The indefiniteness of individuals and the inexactness of classes are both covered by Max Black's useful term 'loose concepts' (Black, 1970, pp. 1 – 13). In many instances, this broader term is more useful and sufficiently analytical for our purposes — differentiating between a case of indefiniteness of individuals and inexactness of classes in some circumstances may not only be difficult but also may contribute little additional to our understanding. The term 'loose concept' was developed by Max Black as a solution to the ancient sorites (heap) sophism. This goes as follows. Every man whose height is one metre is short. Adding one millimetre of height still leaves him short. At each step as a small increment is added, he must be admitted still to be short. There is not one point at which one can logically differentiate and say that a millimetre less makes him short and a millimetre more makes him not-short. But the conclusion is ridiculous — that is, that eventually a man two metres high must be called 'short'. The solution is that the concept of 'shortness' and the concept of 'tallness' are 'loose concepts'. (That is, the classes with 'shortness' or 'tallness' as predicates are inexact classes.) There is no point at which a unique sharp transition can be made from a clear case included within the concept and a borderline case or a case just outside the concept. The class of 'short men' or the class of 'tall men' cannot be sharply demarcated — there are neutral or borderline individuals who can only arbitrarily, and not logically, be assigned within or without the class.

An economic empirical concept and its opposite could be regarded as lying at opposite ends of a spectrum: one can clearly distinguish between both ends but any dividing line drawn between them as they shade into each other can only be arbitrary. Another physical analogy might be that of a lamp bulb shining in the open night: there is a clear distinction between the bright centre of light underneath the bulb and the surrounding darkness but no single clear line of demarcation can be drawn. In other words, the concept and its opposite are distinct, but they are not *discretely* distinct. There is no void between them but a penumbra.

The fact that economics has to work with loose concepts does not mean that calculation is impossible, but it does mean that the results of calculation can be accurate only within certain margins. (We shall return to this very important point from time to time.) As the set of objects being measured increases in number and the coverage spreads from the centre of the class outwards, a demarcation line has to be established arbitrarily on some judgemental basis through the borderline or neutral individuals. Hence, the margins of precision of the numbers must widen. A simple example may help to make this point clear. Assume we have a box full of different coloured glass marbles and we want to ascertain the number of green marbles in the box. At first, the green marbles are easy to pick out — they would be considered 'green' in anyone's judgement. But then we find marbles that vary from having a slight, almost imperceptible tinge of yellow in the green to those that appear mostly yellow with a tinge of green. The same is true of another batch except here the colour involved is blue. In these cases, we have to make an arbitrary judgement for each individual marble whether to classify it as green or yellow or blue. We make our decisions and come up with a number, say that there are 63 green marbles in the box. But the precision of this number does not reflect accurately the imprecision of the underlying reality. To report accurately we would have to report on the number of neutral or borderline cases that we arbitrarily assigned either to this class or out of it: we would need to report something like 63 ± 10. As we shall see, in economic life, movement in time blurs the precision of definition of the 'individuals' or economic entities being measured or counted. Consequently, at some point an arbitrary decision has to be taken as to when the present 'individuals' being measured or counted have changed so much that they can no longer be classed with the original 'individuals'.

In working with subject matter where loose concepts are involved, it is necessary to recognize them and their characteristics. The use of customary methods of logical reasoning forces one to make demarcations in the neutral or borderline cases that are not clear. However, one must recognize that these demarcations are arbitrary or judgemental: there are no logical rules that precisely locate the border lines. As long as one is fully aware of what cases can be considered clear-cut and what cases are borderline, one can reason with loose concepts and reach useful conclusions.

At this point a brief example from economics may serve to illustrate what is meant by a loose concept. We shall discuss the concept of 'unemployment' in more detail later. Here, we may note that the boundaries of the concept of 'unemployment' have to be set or defined arbitrarily when one is to count the number of persons included in the class of 'unemployed'. One cannot logically prove that a person is 'unemployed' if he or she has been without work for, say, 14 days but is still 'employed' if without work for 14 days minus d hours no matter how small a quantity d is defined to be. An arbitrary (and not a logically unique) decision has to be taken about how long a person has to be without work to be considered unemployed. The concept 'employed' shades into the concept 'unemployed' on a continuum, so that while the two opposites are clearly understood there is still no one point in the border area as they shade toward one another where a sharp line should uniquely be drawn between them.

Empirical concepts in economics, in other words, do not appear to obey Aristotle's logical law of the excluded middle: that is, that A must logically be either P or non-P, and there is no middle ground where A can be neither. In economics, in the borderline area, A can be arbitrarily classified as either P or non-P. (Alfred

Marshall, with his emphasis on studying economic reality, was fully aware of this. He commented in the Preface to the first edition of his *Principles*: 'that there is a temptation to classify economic goods in clearly defined groups to gratify the desire for logical precision. But great mischief seems to have been done by yielding to this temptation. . .There is not in real life a clear line of division between things that are and are not Capital, or that are and are not Necessaries or again between labour that is and is not Productive' (Marshall, 1952, p.viii).)

The Phillips curve (i.e. the hypothesis that there is an inverse relationship between the level of unemployment and the rate of changes in wages and prices) is another example of a loose concept. It must be true at the extremes. If resources in an economy are fully employed, any fiscal or monetary stimulus that pumps more purchasing power into the economy cannot result in more output and, therefore, prices must rise. At the other end, when all resources are unemployed, monetary or fiscal stimulus must lead to growth of real output. The difficulty is that in the grey area between the extreme positions, there does not appear to be a fixed unchanging relationship over time between unemployment, prices and fiscal and monetary stimulus.

Most of the numerical data that economists are concerned with are 'estimates', aggregates of 'estimates', index numbers of 'estimates', statistical parameters or mathematical functions calculated from 'estimates'. 'Estimate' in this context is a 'loose concept': the set of individuals or objects being measured or counted is not perfectly homogenous and, consequently, neither the number resulting from the measurement nor the measurement process is unique. It is perfectly possible for some other classification procedure to be applied just as logically and some other number to be obtained. The important point is that the 'estimate' is not an approximation: a precise 'true value' does not exist.

Here we might explore the example of commodities in the attempt to make this point more explicit. Most commodity statistics, no matter how precisely stated, are 'estimates' of a loose concept. They measure some class of 'individual' that is not perfectly definite or homogeneous. Even a commodity like raw cotton is made up of many different fibre lengths and grades. The partitioning of the cotton into the various classes is inevitably discretionary or arbitrary. When aggregate statistics of output or consumption are given, it is necessary to assign weights to the different grades or lengths to derive manageable aggregate figures. When it comes to industrial commodities, the varieties of a product come in bewildering number and forcing them into statistical classes is even more arbitrary.

As we shall see in the discussion on cost – benefit analysis, it is extremely difficult or impossible to identify a single price for a commodity class in one market location, much less over several markets. Usually there is a whole collection of prices correspon- ding to different sets of quality (and sometimes also quantity) specifications of the commodity and to the different packages of services that are bundled with the commodity. List prices quoted often differ from transactions prices, which may vary from tran- saction to transaction. The result is often that, when one is talking about 'the price' of a commodity, one is really talking about some kind of an average or an index number over quality specifications, services bundle, markets, and time.

The prices of services are even more difficult to handle. Even pricing a single individual service transaction may run up against the problem of indefiniteness of what constitutes an 'individual' — that is, defining sharply the appropriate measurement unit for a transaction. A good example is health care, where the appropriate unit of output may be taken to be 'a cure'. Appendicitis is now often treated with drugs, whereas formerly an operation was precribed; though the cost of treatment now is less there is greater probability of a ruptured appendix. A cure thus may have multiple characteristics, and to price a cure requires information about con- sumers' evaluation of the trade-offs among the different characteristics, this may depend on economic variables such as in- come, relative prices, as well as tastes (Triplett, 1975, p. 45).

More generally, when one is working with estimates of loose concepts and not true values, one's mind set has to be different. We need to think not in terms of an exact figure precisely pinning a phenomenon to a point but more in terms of a blob or a piece of putty covering our object. Or, if one's mind runs this way, one can picture our data as being like a net capturing a wriggling phenomenon within it.

Most modern economists ignore this whole set of problems and blithely calculate with abandon. Most perceptive econometricians, realizing that economics cannot be exact, introduce the stochastic element of a random unmeasurable variable (or 'disturbance') into their equations. This is justifiable in cases where the errors are sufficiently numerous, diverse *and* small so that the differences between the model and reality could in practical terms be regarded as the results of random variables. This solution may well be adequate for many, perhaps most, micro problems. But, as the problem to be dealt with becomes more aggregative, the limitations of accuracy of the data, the change in structure, in precision of definition of individuals and in meaning of concepts over time, the use of 'loose' concepts beyond their boundary states, the fuzziness of some aspects of economic reality and the major impact of unforeseeable events — all these cannot be handled by adding a 'disturbance' factor to the equations. What is necessary is to approach the problem (or to set up the model) in a way that recognizes explicitly the roughness or the degree of imprecision of the parameters and of the variables themselves.

In chapter 5, I cite the case of the inability of the national accounts to provide a logically satisfactory measure of output for government services, some non-governmental services, etc. Kenneth Arrow has endorsed the findings by Stone and Prais (1952) that the construction of a complete set of national accounts in real terms can never be carried through with complete consistency (Arrow, 1974b, p. 4). In their article, Stone and Prais show that expressing aggregates of goods and non-factor services in terms of constant prices (by deflating nominal prices through a price index) is in principle simple and feasible. *But this is not true* for unilateral transactions, such as taxes and transfers, and financial transactions, such as saving and lending. (For example, when a deflator for saving has to be used, it might seem right to use the deflator for consumption on the grounds that the saver had the choice of spending his income on consumption. But if this is done, the deflated values of consumption and saving will no longer be equal to the deflated value of income. The deflated accounts will balance only if saving is deflated by the deflator appropriate to real asset formation. But this is essentially an arbitrary choice.) Transactions in factor services are also for practical reasons in this category unless some means can be found of measuring and pricing them. Since all of these transactions enter into the national accounts, the question then is whether the national accounts as a whole can be expressed in prices of another period and still continue to balance. Stone and Prais conclude that a simple solution can be found but that it is arbitrary — and should be recognized as such (Stone and Prais, 1952, pp. 566 – 7).

Robert Dorfman (1975) in a brilliant commentary has shown that the economics of pollution constitute a third set of problems that the national accounts structure is not able to grasp precisely. He points out that there is a built-in perversity in the GNP accounts. For example, air pollution controls may reduce medical bills, laundry bills and building maintenance: they reduce GNP as measured in the same proportion that they increase economic welfare. Also, while the cost increases imposed on the polluting industries for taking measures to reduce pollution are included, the cost savings to industries resulting from cleaner air (citriculture and building maintenance) and cleaner water (shell fishing and intake treatment costs) are not identified or measured. Dorfman believes that it will be impossible ever to construct mathematical models that will tell us *exactly* what the socially desirable levels and distribution of pollution should be. We cannot rank alternative pollution-control programmes by means of mathematical models because there is no satisfactory way to measure the social cost of pollution or to value the external effects and public goods involved: '. . . I do not see that this impediment will yield to "further research" or other of the standard cures' (Dorfman, 1975, p. 254).

Lester C. Thurow maintains that economics does not have an effective theory of inflation because it does not have a deterministic theory of oligopolistic behaviour that can explain price behaviour in such markets. An increasingly larger fraction of GNP is being produced in sectors that are either not competitive (e.g. government, medicine) or where there are only a few competitors. In spite of the spate of work that was done on this latter problem a few decades ago, no deterministic price theory emerged such as existed for competitive firms or individuals. In the work on oligopoly, realistic sets of assumptions always led to indeterminant results. Deterministic solutions required assumptions counter to the facts. The world is not a two-person zero-sum game, and no oligopolist expects competitors to hold their prices or quantities fixed in response to his decisions. But these are the assumptions required to lead to deterministic results. Thurow concludes that if prices are indeterminant in oligopolist situations, then economics cannot have a useful theory of inflation (Thurow, 1977, p. 92).

Thurow is unquestionably right in identifying the impossibility of developing a deterministic theory of oligopoly that can be shown to lead to unique precise and accurate results. But this is too high a demand to be made of economic theory — it is judging economics by the standards of physics, which works with sharp and not loose concepts. Economics can have 'useful' theories that do not meet this impossibly high standard.

Another example of the difficulty economics has in finding concepts that can grasp the real world with precise measurement is Hollis Chenery's and Lance Taylor's study of development patterns. They concluded that, at least among small countries, natural resource differences have a major impact on growth rates even though there is no single statistically feasible and theoretically satisfactory criterion for classifying countries according to resource endowments (Chenery and Taylor, 1968, p. 396).

Loose concepts over time

The real meaning of the 'loose concept' approach becomes much easier to grasp when it is observed in action over time. Because the very structure of economic reality is in flux, we can observe how what is straddled by the boundaries of a concept shifts or how the 'individuals', the entities or objects observed lose in definitiveness over time. This phenomenon is probably most familiar in the so-called index number dilemma: if the coverage of items is revised over time, the index number loses its usefulness for recording change over time; if the coverage remains constant, the index number loses its relevance to the present. (In an ideal and true cost of living index, the commodities and service covered would be replaced as necessary over time with new minimum cost items that are exactly equivalent in terms of the consumer's own preferences to the original items purchased in the base period. Such an index cannot, however, be computed in the real world.) Economists are accustomed to finding a band of indeterminateness when measuring price changes between the results of using a Laspeyre index — weighting by quantities of the first period — and the results of using a Paasche index — weighting by quantities of the second period.

Since the location of the boundaries of an inexact class is arbitrary, the classifications of economic phenomena (e.g. commodities or industries) are made differently by different observers and over time. This is not only a question of differing decisions by the observers, but, more importantly, *it is the underlying reality that is changing*: the 'individuals' being observed are indefinite in their time dimension. Changes in the resources and techniques used, new products produced and the changing demands met totally transform whole sectors of the economy.

This was one of the principal observations that Leontief called to the attention of the profession in his presidential address to the American Econmic Association:

> In contrast to most physical sciences, we study a system that is not only exceedingly complex but is also in a state of constant flux. I have in mind not the obvious change in the variables, such as outputs, prices or levels of employment, that our equations are supposed to explain, but the basic structural relationships described by the form and the parameters of these equations. (Leontief, 1971, p. 3)

Leontief went on to praise agricultural economics as an exceptional example of a healthy balance between theoretical and empirical analysis. The subsequent comments of James T. Bonnen (1975) in his presidential address to the American Agricultural Economics Association on exactly this problem of trying to capture an economy where reality is escaping from the concepts set up in the past are especially pertinent therefore. Bonnen pointed out that there was a growing obsolescence in the concepts of 'individuals' that the data system attempted to measure. The 'family farm' constitutes the central concept around which three-quarters of our food and fibre statistics are designed and collected. Yet it has become an increasingly obsolete representation of the sector. In many cases, contracting and vertical integration of both inputs and outputs have undermined, if not destroyed, the traditional concept of the farm. Years ago, counting population on farms and calling it *farm population* made some sense. But today, the concept of a 'farm population' is practically meaningless. Besides the difficulty in defining a farm, many farmers do not live on their own or other farms; much agricultural labour also does not live on a farm; and there are many people residing on farms who are not employed in agriculture.

Carolyn Shaw Bell has called attention to a similar shift in the reality covered by the concept of a 'typical family' in US statistics. Bureau of Labor Statistics figures are given for a 'worker with three dependents' in the series on family or household income and family budgets, whereas today this type of family makes up only a tiny minority of the population (Bell, 1977, pp. 44 – 5).

Unemployment

The concept of 'unemployment' is meant to provide a basis for an estimate of the availability of labour for employment and an indicator of the economic hardships of the workers without jobs. While the concept in more developed countries still does serve these uses as in the past, it does not do so in the same measure and the same meaning. The US labour force is now different in composition from the past. Only two-fifths are still the once preponderant male adult heads of family. The rest are women (some heads of household, some holding 'second jobs' of the family, some available for part-time work only); officially retired people, who are available for part-time work, up to the income level at which their earnings reduce their state pension; some young adults genuinely looking for work; some young adults who prefer to alternate between employment and 'unemployment' when they draw tax-free unemployment benefit; unemployables registered for 'employment' in order to be eligible for welfare payments and food stamps; and full-time students who are available for part-time work only.

For a small minority of workers, 'unemployment' is regarded as a positive advantage. They work only long enough to secure unemployment benefit coverage — the period of unemployment is the real objective. This is true of some artists, for example, for whom the period of 'unemployment' is when they do their real work. In an artists' colony like Provincetown, 'unemployment' regularly rises to around 50 per cent during the winter months. Before unemployment benefit was taxed, a 1979 US Government Accounting Office study found that some workers collected unemployment benefit that was at times higher than their normal after-tax income.

It is clear that many unemployed are above the poverty line and are able to decide on taking longer to search for jobs that will provide greater job satisfaction to pay. The large number of households with more than one wage-earner means that the loss of one job for them is no longer so disastrous.

On the other hand, workers who want a job but do not look for one because they believe the search will fail are classified as 'discouraged workers', are not counted as 'unemployed' and are also not included in the labour force. There were well over 1 million such persons in the United States in the first quarter of 1983, for example. If the economic outlook suddenly brightened, the first result might be a sudden temporary increase in 'unemployment' as the discouraged workers flock into the job market. There are also many employed people who have earnings that do not provide an adequate standard of living.

The current system of employment insurance in the United States provides an incentive for employers to increase the number of temporary lay-offs. Martin Feldstein's estimates imply that the incentive provided by the current average level of unemployment insurance benefits is responsible for approximately one-half of temporary lay-off unemployment (Feldstein, 1978, p. 834). (Temporary lay-offs have accounted for about 50 per cent of unemployment spells of all persons classified as 'unemployed job losers'.)

Peter Drucker (1978) has concluded that the traditional unemployment index for the United States has become meaningless and misleading. Without going as far as this, it is reasonable to conclude that the unemployment concept in the more developed countries like the United States does not precisely cover the persons who are able to and want to work and who are experiencing economic hardship. In short, while 'unemployment' remains an indispensable concept for economic analysis and policy, it is a loose concept that provides only a rough measure of the phenomenon it is intended to grasp.

In less developed countries, it is now well accepted that 'unemployment' is something quite different from the Great Depression concept or from the present-day reality in more developed countries. Essentially, the 'unemployed' in the cities of the less developed countries are in large part people who have migrated to the city because their incomes in the city while 'unemployed' are greater than their subsistence incomes in the countryside would have been. The urban incomes of the 'unemployed' are derived from useful petty trade and backyard industry as well as from begging, selling unwanted services (i.e. watching parked cars — if you refuse the service, your tyres may be slashed), thieving, living on richer members of the extended family, etc). This income, plus the probability of eventually finding regular employment in the city, is sufficiently high to maintain a continuous supply of 'unemployed' in the city during the process of development. As development proceeds, eventually the countryside is sufficiently depopulated so that 'unemployment' becomes more like that historically known in the older industrial countries. (This is a summary comment on a complex phenomenon first noted by A. M. Kamarck. Similar conclusions were later independently arrived at by Arnold Harberger, 1972, and by Michael Todaro, 1969.)

In many less developed countries the social and economic organization is such that the lines between 'employment' and 'non-employment' and 'participation' and 'non-participation' in the labour force are not merely blurred but even non-existent for many people. In Indonesia, women whose main occupation is housekeeping are classified as outside the labour force even though over 1 million of them work outside the home in paid employment for 20 or more hours a week, while women who do no housekeeping and have fewer hours of paid employment are classified as being in the labour force. Since there is no unemployment benefit, the very poorest people are the working people who by one means or another desperately secure enough income to stay alive. Many of the 'unemployed', on the other hand, are persons who have some education or training and are being supported by their households while they wait for a high-paying job to open up. In terms of availability for employment, the 'unemployed' with means of support are often less available than the very poor who are barely surviving with some kind of 'job'. In terms of welfare, many of the unemployed are living better than those classified as employed (Bruton, 1978, pp. 52 – 3).

Markets

John Hicks, in a remarkable preface to a recent book, has called attention to the fact that there has been a major shift in the boundaries of the basic concept of 'market' in the real world (1977, p.xi). In the past, the dominant market form in the economy had been what he calls *flexprice* markets, that is, mostly unorganized markets with prices made by merchant intermediaries and responsive to supply and demand, but also including some organized markets likewise responsive to supply and demand. Today, the dominant markets are what he calls *fix-price*, in which prices are set by the producers (or by some authority) and are *not* determined by supply and demand. Changes in costs and demand affect the prices that are fixed; but these changes do not automatically change the prices. Price decisions have to be made deliberately, and are influenced by many other things than supply and demand.

Money supply

'Money supply' has in recent years become regarded by many people as a key factor in national policy. The aggregate figures on money supply are watched carefully — governments are criticized or praised, the financial markets go up or down, when the annual rate of growth of the money supply changes by a few tenths of 1 per cent from one week to another. In the week ending 10 October, 1979, the US Federal Reserve Board announced that the basic money supply, M1, had increased by $2.8 billion, i.e. less than 1 per cent. As no increase had been expected, there was near panic selling of securities, and paper losses of as much as $65 billion resulted. Two weeks later, the Federal Reserve Board admitted that a reporting error was responsible for the increase shown and that the true figure showed a tiny *decrease*. This set off a buying spree!

Accuracy in reporting is clearly important, but the problems stemming from the looseness of economic concepts are at least as important in the case of 'money supply'. At the same time as the monetarist economic approach was becoming increasingly influential, the accepted concept of basic money supply was becoming less and less relevant. In fact, while the basic money supply, M1, no longer had the same meaning as in the past, the same was true of the other measures of broader money stocks, M2 – M5, which included time and savings deposits and other near-money categories. If one accepts the usual definition of money as a 'commonly accepted means of payment', what appears to have happened is that a growing number of different kinds of means of payment were not captured by the M1 series at all and largely escaped the other measures too: NOW (negotiable orders of withdrawal) accounts at savings banks that in everything but name are current accounts; automatic transfer savings accounts (ATS) at commercial banks that make these funds as easily spendable as the balances in current accounts; the widespread credit cards, which increasingly substitute for currency; 'money market funds' on which cheques can be drawn without notice; 'repos' (repurchase agreements) or 'deposit-sweeping accounts' under which a depositor keeps a zero or a fixed minimum current account balance at a bank (whenever the balance exceeds the specified amount, the excess is 'swept' into an income-earning asset on a daily or weekly basis; whenever the balance falls below the minimum, funds are automatically transferred back).

During 1981, NOW accounts spread from New England throughout the United States and the old M1 measure consequently showed a *drop* of 7 per cent on the preceding year while nominal GNP *rose* by 9 per cent. Trying to keep M1 relevant, the central bank redefined the measure to include NOW accounts and some of the other new transactions accounts. (The new M1 includes currency in circulation plus demand deposits at commercial banks — excluding demand deposits held by foreign banks and official institutions — plus other accounts on which cheques can be written at all depository institutions, including NOW accounts, automatic transfer accounts, credit union share drafts and demand deposits at mutual savings banks.) The two measures give very different pictures of what is happening to 'money supply': in January 1982, old M1 grew by $1.3 billion while new M1 grew by over four times as much.

The change from the one to the other measure also means that today's money market supply figures no longer correspond exactly to the money supply measures of the past and past relationships of the money supply aggregates to nominal GNP can therefore be only roughly relevant for the future. The new M1 still has problems. It does not cover the deposit-sweeping or repo accounts. Money supply figures are calculated on the basis of balances at the end of the business day. In these types of accounts only the unswept balance enters into the figures of the basic money supply, M1. But the depositor for all practical purposes regards some part or all of the swept amounts as included in his holdings of money. Money market funds on which cheques can be drawn are also not included in M1 because it is felt that people regard these accounts more as savings than as transactions balances. In reality, however, this may vary from person to person or even from day to day for the same person. It is evident that large shifts will continue to take place in the ways people hold their financial assets as financial innovation persists.

Finally, there is still another factor that is usually overlooked in discussions of measurement of money supply that is as important for the United States today as it was for Great Britain in earlier periods. The US dollar is an international currency and increasingly large sums are held and used abroad. An OECD study of the underground economy (referred to in the next chapter) points out that because of this fact it is meaningless to relate changes in US currency outstanding to US GNP. The other components of M1, transactions balances, also are affected by international influences and not simply by activity in the United States. There is a highly integrated worldwide financial market and an increasing number of corporations from all countries have access to it. This means that measures of money supply in all the industrial countries may overlook the foreign transactions balances available to their citizens. A corporation refused a loan from a bank branch in New York because of American credit restrictions may simply have its headquarters in London borrow from the same bank's branch in London or Frankfurt.

As a result of factors such as these, it is increasingly evident that we cannot expect to be able to measure money supply aggregates with any kind of precision. And, correspondingly, attempting to measure the relationship of money supply aggregates in a single country to its economic activity or GNP in any more than a rough way is also more and more futile. The illusion that central bank policy could be simplified to picking a money supply target and holding the economy to it is just that, an illusion. The task is more complex and there are no simple mechanical measures to rely on or simple rules to follow. Charles Goodhart, the chief monetary adviser to the Bank of England, perhaps has summarized the experience with the loose concept of money supply best in the new 'law' he formulated: Any measure of the money supply that is adopted as a guide to official policy promptly loses its meaning (*Economist*, 1981).

Similar problems have arisen with the boundaries of the existing concepts of the 'banking system' and 'financial institution'. The senior financial officer of Sears, Roebuck, the world's largest retailer, now describes Sears as being mainly a 'financial institution'. Earnings from Sears' insurance operations, brokerage fees, retail credit and savings and loan association surpass the earnings from selling commodities. The General Electric Credit Corporation, which once existed solely to help sell General Electric home appliances, is now the third largest diversified finance company. In the USA, Walter Wriston, head of Citicorp, the second largest US bank, has said that the ideal bank of the future already exists and it is called Merill Lynch Pierce Fenner and Smith, the largest securities firm in the USA. This firm now offers current accounts, deposit-sweeping accounts, personal loans, savings-type investments and credit cards but is not classified as a commercial bank.

Transaction costs

Finally, because of the incessant change in the underlying reality, the inability of loose concepts to partition reality sharply and uniquely and the economic forces that work against accuracy in reporting, economics is confronted with two problems that are of minor or no consequence for the physical sciences: it often costs more to get the facts than it costs to make the decision in question, or the investigation to get the facts takes so long that the question has to be settled or settles itself before the results are available. The need to take into account transactional costs (including the costs of delaying the decision) of securing better data in most economic decisions means that in many, if not most, instances the probable marginal gain from better data will be matched by the marginal transactional cost of getting such data while the available data are still quite rough, incomplete and imprecise.

This problem pervades the economic system: in every market all participants have to ascertain just what the market price really is. George Stigler (1961) points out that, except in a completely centralized market, price dispersion at any one moment is ubiquitous even for relatively homogeneous goods. Consequently, any buyer or seller who wishes to find the most favourable price must spend time and effort in a search for it. Because of this cost, which is necessary to overcome ignorance, it is not normally profitable for buyers or sellers to eliminate all dispersion of prices: conditions of supply and demand change; new buyers and sellers come into every market; the cost of keeping currently informed about the market for all articles that an individual buys or a seller sells is prohibitive. All this is true of homogeneous products; when qualitative differences enter in, the cost of overcoming ignorance is even greater. In less developed countries where bazaar and peasant markets are important, Clifford Geertz (1978) has shown that the search for information is the central activity of the market. The primary problem facing the participants in the market is not choosing among options but finding out what they really are.

Similar problems exist in finding profitable investments for capital and the most remunerative jobs for workers. By undertaking a sufficient cost, the effects of ignorance upon people can be kept within tolerable bounds, but it would be uneconomic to try to eliminate it all (Stigler, 1961, p. 224). In brief, in economic transactions, it is usually necessary (and economic) to operate with actual prices that may differ by a considerable margin from the precise price the theoretical market-clearing equation is supposed to determine.

In the physical sciences, it is accepted that, given an absence of bias, sequences of measured values approach the ideal of 'true value' insofar as that ideal can be revealed through measurement. It is also accepted that perfectly exact measurement of the true value is not attainable and, therefore, careful scientific practice is to state results of measurement with margins of possible error. We have seen that in economics, however, we cannot start with the assumption of an absence of bias but rather have to start with an enquiry into the human forces that may be distorting the information available and that may contribute to errors during the process of data collection. In this chapter, I have tried to show that in economics only arbitrarily (or by idealizing reality) can we work with concepts of definite, unchangeable individuals and exact classes. The economic reality our economic concepts are groping to grasp cannot be pinned down exactly and can be quantified or measured exactly only within margins of precision.

5

National Income and Product Accounts

For so it is, oh Lord my God, I measure it; but what it is that I measure I do not know.

St Augustine, *Confessions*

In macroeconomics, imprecision of concept (indefiniteness of individuals, and inexactitude of classes that concepts refer to) is inherent in large sectors of the economy. (There are also, of course, problems of inaccuracy arising in the collection and processing of data, but these can be minimized, within limits, by greater efforts, by better techniques, etc.) Earlier, the discussion referred to the findings of Stone and Prais (1952) that the construction of a set of national accounts in real terms is only possible on an arbitrary basis and to Robert Dorfman's findings (1972) that the national accounts cannot satisfactorily measure the economics of pollution. There are other important elements of imprecision in the national accounts. Roughly, these accounts fall into a hierarchy of preciseness. Measurement of the output of primary products is most precisely accurate because these products tend to be generally uniform or change only slowly in quality over time and they are usually sold in ways that come closest to the economist's concept of perfect markets. Manufactures, or secondary products, tend to be more changeable in quality over time and their markets are much less perfect. Finally, in services, quality may vary from transaction to transaction, the markets are highly fragmented and it may be difficult or impossible to measure the output at all.

Measurement of the true output and productivity in some kinds of commodity production (e.g. defence items), in some services provided by non-residential business, and especially in the services provided by general government, households and non-profit institutions, is generally recognized by social accountants as impossible. There seems to be a difference of opinion as to why this is so in government services (e.g. our inability to identify the physical content of the particular government service to be rendered or in the price per unit to assign to it) but none as to the fact. After surveying six alternative approaches to determining real output of the educational system, Alice Rivlin found them all wanting (Moss, 1973a, pp. 14 – 15).

General government, households and non-profit organizations do not sell their output, so no proper measure of their output can be constructed. Instead, net output, i.e. the amount left over after deducting purchases from business, is usually estimated by the convention that net output moves like full-time equivalent employment. There is an additional measurement difference: no return to capital and land and no depreciation are counted, and no indirect taxes are levied on the compensation of employees. Consequently, the figures for labour earnings also measure national income, net national product and gross national product (Denison, 1973, p. 23).

Denison points out that *we know nothing* about changes in the 'amount' of 'products' such as national defence, education, etc., that governments and non-profit organizations provide to individuals by use of the resources that they buy (Denison, 1973, p. 23). The National Bureau of Economic Research commented, after reviewing certain characteristics of the health industry (consumer ignorance, reliance on the medical profession for information on the quality and quantity of the product to be purchased, restrictions on competition in the medical profession, the role of need and third-party payment for health services), that, as a result, 'output' of the industry cannot simply be taken as equivalent to expenditures (NBER, 1972, p. 4).

These economic sectors where exact measurement of output has been found to be impossible cover an increasingly important portion of total output. In education, health, police protection, fire protection, the administration of justice and much of construction, what is counted as 'output' in the accounts is really a cost of inputs index. It has been impossible to devise satisfactory and independent measures of the outputs produced in these areas (Juster, 1973, p. 71).

There are similar difficulties in measuring output in other service industries. It is always difficult to measure the impact of quality changes in output but this is particularly troublesome in the service industries and for understanding the growth of their output and productivity. In the trade sector, the growth of the supermarket has resulted in the customer using his own labour to find and collect the commodities he is buying, rather than the retail clerk doing this as before. This must have some impact on our earlier concept and measurement of input. The customer may also be getting some additional output by enjoying the opportunity to survey the whole range of goods on display (Fabricant, 1972, p. 3). Another example of the same problem: by 1983, most of the petrol sold in the US was put in car tanks by the customers themselves from self-service pumps, compared to practically none a decade earlier.

While measurement in the primary commodity-producing sectors is undoubtedly easier than in the manufacturing and service sectors, the former have some problems too. Bonnen has pointed out that farm income figures are a good example of conceptual obsolescence: moving the beef and dairy cattle inventory changes from current income to capital account (where it should be) would have reduced 1973 net farm income by almost a quarter (Bonnen, 1975, p. 755).

In manufacturing output, there is the question how accurate the price deflators can be over time. Usually prices are reported for consumer commodities or fixed specifications. However, new commodities continually appear that are more or less substitutes for existing ones and existing commodities change in quality. (This is another example of indefiniteness of individuals — how much change must take place before Commodity A must be considered to have become Commodity B?) Price indexes can only roughly and imperfectly cope with this problem. Statisticians calculating price indexes of durable goods generally do not even try to cope with these practically insuperable problems but prepare indexes that merely reflect changes in cost of production without much regard to changes in their productive performance (R. Ruggles, 1959, pp. 93 – 4).

It will be recalled that GNP estimates also cover subsistence output (including household activities — cooking, cleaning, etc.) very poorly, both in the less developed and in more developed countries. There is a vast literature on this subject that does not have to be cited here. For our purposes we need only to remember that (a) no matter how subsistence activities are covered or omitted, the results are still unsatisfactory and at best indicate only orders of magnitude; and (b) the size and the composition of the subsistence sectors change considerably in the process of economic development of the less developed countries and in the evolution of industrialized societies.

The measurement of income in the national accounts has other special problems: the income tax system provides incentives to the tax-payer to classify as much as possible of his receipts (which increase his command over the use of society's scarce resources) in non-taxable categories or as capital gains rather than income. Richard M. Titmuss (1962) has shown in devastating detail how inaccurate and inadequate official income statistics have been in the United Kingdom. It is unlikely that the figures in other countries are greatly superior.

An important gap in the estimates is of the elusive income-in-kind received by officials and middle and upper employees of corporations and other organizations in countries that have a strongly progressive income tax structure. Individuals in this category often receive large portions of their income (unreported and untaxed) in the form of the use of 'company' cars, flats, hotel accommodation, yachts, travel and entertainment (restaurants, golf courses, night clubs, theatre). What this means is that income-in-kind does not figure in the national accounts as income but rather as intermediate costs of production, and GDP is accordingly underestimated. No statistical studies of corporate income-in-kind appear to exist. The OECD's National Accounts Division, with the help of the statistical offices of the OECD countries (all the non-communist industrialized countries), made a comprehensive investigation into the underground economy (OECD, 1982a). While it found studies made by employer groups of low-level employees' income-in-kind, i.e. pilfering or employee theft or 'fiddles', no comparable information has been produced on the income-in-kind enjoyed by middle and upper management. The OECD assumes that this latter income is 'unlikely to be quantitatively significant'. This assumption could be correct, but any wide acquaintance with the corporate way of life calls it into question. There are also bits of evidence scattered around that appear to reinforce one's doubts. The British Institute of Management reported that, in 1979, 60 to

70 per cent of all new cars sold in Great Britain were 'company cars' (Borders, 1979, p. D1). In Japan, the direct charges to corporation expense accounts alone are reported by the National Tax Administration to exceed total national expenditures on education or on national defence. In the United States, any attempt to reduce the tax write-off of expense account expenditures on meals provokes irresistible reaction by corporate interests as well as by the restaurant industry, who see this as a direct threat to their survival. According to the NY State Restaurant Association, one-quarter of all meals bought in New York City are on expense account (Serrin, 1981, p. F15). In 1982, a tax reform proposal that entered the American legislative process as a limitation on the tax write-off of expense account meals was transformed into a device to reduce tax evasion on the tips received by waiters and waitresses.

Statistical data are equally difficult to obtain on similar practices in the centrally planned countries, and revealing glimpses occur even more rarely in the domestic press. There are enough indications, however, that it is fairly safe to assume that income-in-kind 'perks' are at least as important for the top government and industrial bureaucrats as they are in the mixed economies of the industrial countries and the third world. Nowhere, however, is it a part of measured national income. To an appreciable extent it would be impossible to measure it precisely if the attempt were made: how much of an expense account lunch contributes only to the well-being of the particular individual consuming it and how much is a legitimate cost of getting business? Certainly, it would be possible to conceive that the sum of these two could be either more than 100 per cent of the price paid (in the case of an excellent lunch) or less than 100 per cent (in the case of a mediocre meal).

There are at least three other sectors that in most countries partly or wholly escape the national accounts: (i) the non-criminal 'underground economy' of legally acceptable services and commodities that are exchanged for cash 'off-the-book' (as the revealing popular phrase puts it) to avoid income tax or national insurance contributions or to continue receiving unemployment benefit or state retirement pensions; (ii) illegal or criminal activities; and (iii) a growing barter economy.

In recent years, people have become aware of the underground economy. Various adjectives have been used to describe it, such as 'black', 'dual', 'hidden', 'parallel', etc., and the activities covered are not always exactly the same. Here, we shall restrict it to economic activities that are non-criminal *per se* but that at least one of the parties involved tries to hide from governmental notice.

A number of partial studies of the underground economy have been made in the United States. The Internal Revenue Service, initially openly sceptical that this economy was of significant proportions, finally concluded that, for, the year 1976, 6 – 9 per cent of legal sector incomes of individuals was unreported. This was an absolute amount of \$75 – 100 billion or an income around the size of that of the Netherlands or Brazil — and considerably greater than that of India. The IRS estimated that as much as one-half of rents and royalties, over one-third of income from self-employment and one-fifth of capital gains went unreported (US Congress, 1980).

In the United Kingdom, Sir William Pile, the chairman of Inland Revenue, told the House of Commons in 1979 that tax evasion through cash payments could amount to as much as 7½ per cent of GNP. The government statisticians, estimating total income from family expenditure surveys and from direct estimates of income, found the gap between the two had grown from under 1 per cent of GDP in the 1960s to almost 4 per cent by the mid 1970s (Economist, 1980a). The two figures (7½ and 4 per cent) are not necessarily contradictory: the spending data are incomplete and the direct income estimates are not calculated only from tax returns. Farmers' incomes, estimated from the Ministry of Agriculture's production figures, result in a much higher figure of farm income than the farmer incomes declared on tax returns.

In Italy, there is a saying 'laws are for foreigners and law students'. Labour and tax laws apply mainly to employees of the great state and private enterprises. Small firms and individual entrepreneurs live mostly in what the Italians call the 'submerged economy'. They pay few or no taxes, ignore employment legislation and employ many of the officially unemployed workers. In Argentina, the 'black' transactions are credited with making it possible for people to survive the recurring triple-digit inflations and frequent devaluations.

When one puts together the extensive evasion of income tax by the self-employed, the small enterprise sector and recipients of rent, royalty, dividends and interest income on the one hand, and the non-taxed income-in-kind paid to employees by organizations, on the other hand, it appears that the income tax may be becoming a tax on honesty and on cash wages. Income estimates derived from tax data, consequently, may be becoming more measures of these than of total personal incomes in the United States, United Kingdom and elsewhere.

There is also an underground or 'parallel' economy in the Eastern European countries, particularly in services. In Hungary, the official party daily newspaper *Napazabadsog* has admitted that 70 – 75 per cent of all Hungarian families get at least part of their income from the 'second' or 'unregistered' economy. The government no longer attempts to suppress this type of activity but allows it to exist (*Economist*, 1980b). In Czechoslovakia, the authorities contemplated restoring free enterprise for artisans and so on. The artisans themselves opposed the proposal. Under the present system, their official wages give them security; their tools and materials are supplied free by the state, and they earn untaxed money by doing unofficial work during or outside regular working hours.

The OECD study on the underground economy (1982a) mentioned above tried to evaluate the extent to which the national account calculations in different countries did allow for economic activities that were unreported in the tax returns. Where the national accounts are built up on production and expenditure data from a sector, for example, an individual may succeed in concealing some income from the tax collector but the information on the sector as whole will be more accurate. Also, the statistical offices using tax data make explicit upward adjustments where possible, based on the results of tax audits, to allow for under-reporting. In the United States, the national accounts Personal Income estimate was $23 billion (or 15 per cent) higher in 1947 than the comparable Internal Revenue figure of $149.7 billion. In 1978, the national accounts figure was $103.5 billion (or 8 per cent) higher than the IRS $1302 billion. The difference between the two figures is supposed to be a rough measure of non-compliance with the tax code. The estimated decrease in percentage of non-compliance from 1947 to 1978 is somewhat surprising, however (Park, 1981).

With all the corrections that can be made to the national accounts to try to cover unreported activities, there is inevitably an element of guesswork, and it is generally felt that the adjustments tend to be understated. The US statisticians estimated that in 1976 the accounts caught unreported legal production equivalent to around 1.5 per cent of GNP but omitted unreported legal activities equivalent to under 1.0 per cent of recorded GNP. (The OECD study demolishes one basis for the very large estimates — 10 – 20 per cent of GNP — that have been made by some economists of the size of the underground economy in the United States, arguing from the growth in recent years in the ratio of currency in circulation to GNP. Since US currency is used internationally, relating its circulation to the size of the US GNP alone is not valid.) For the United Kingdom, the study quotes estimates for unreported legal activities that are not included in GDP ranging from 1.0 to 4.7 per cent of GDP in 1977, with the OECD giving more credence to the lower figures. Less information is available about other countries. For Italy, estimates are quoted ranging from 4.0 to 20.0 per cent for 1976. While the OECD discounts the higher figures, it does comment that the very large revisions recently made to the official series '. . .highlight the degree of uncertainty surrounding the true size of Italy's GPD' (1982a, p. 36).

The underground economy fuzzes not only the total GNP figures but also some of the components. For example, in the United States there was a great deal of concern because the official Commerce Department figures showed a considerable drop in the personal savings rate. Even after later revision upwards, the rate still shows a drop from 8.0 per cent of disposable personal income in 1970 to 6.4 per cent in 1981 (1982, p. 13). However, the Federal Reserve's independent estimate, which is more likely to catch underground income (since it is based on reports of monetary inflows to financial institutions and estimated household holdings of cash), indicates instead that the personal savings rate *increased* from 9 per cent in 1970 to 10 per cent in 1981 (Board of Governors, 1983). In other words, the rate probably did not really change significantly over the decade and there was no need for alarm.

Crime, i.e. activities that are illegal *per se*, is not normally covered in the GNP accounts. In the United States, the Internal Revenue Service estimates that around 10 per cent of income from crime is reported on tax returns and so gets into the national accounts. In Italy, the accounts include estimates made of income from the smuggling and subsequent domestic distribution of cigarettes. Stealing or forcible transfer of property does not add to gross national product in any case. This is not true of all other crime (e.g. illegal gambling, prostitution, illegal drugs), which may contribute to the purchaser's utility by providing the illegal services or commodities he desires. If one could assume that crime was a small and stable proportion of GNP, the lack of coverage would not matter. This, however, is probably not the case, at least in the United States. The IRS has estimated that in 1977 the total incomes not reported on tax returns of individuals from illegal gambling, drug sales and prostitution amounted to $30 billion, equivalent to around 1½ per cent of GNP (U.S. Congress, 1980, p. 8).

The IRS estimates do not include estimates of income from thefts from business. These losses are deducted as costs by business corporations but the income to the thieves is not included in their reported incomes; GNP is consequently understated. The US Chamber of Commerce in 1974 estimated that the total losses from white-collar crime in the public and private sectors were over $40 billion yearly, i.e. almost 3 per cent of GNP (U.S. Congress, 1980, p. 35). US Department of Commerce estimates for the same year covering a somewhat different set of categories came to only 1 per cent of GNP (OECD, 1982a, p. 39). Both figures are, of course, hardly more than informed guesses. Other types of income not included in the IRS estimates were: arson for profit, smuggling goods other than drugs, bootlegging of cigarettes, production and sale of illegal copies of tapes, films and records.

During Prohibition in the United States illegal distilling and brewing, bootlegging, speakeasies and rum-running were quite important activities and particularly important economically for certain border regions and sea-oriented areas like Cape Cod and South Florida. These activities would have been left out of the accounts until suddenly, with Prohibition's repeal, they became legal. Similarly, in recent years the growing, smuggling, transport and trade in marijuana and cocaine must be growth industries and economically significant in a number of areas. In Florida, the drug trade rivals or surpasses tourism as a source of income. The illegal earnings from export of marijuana from Colombia were estimated by its attorney-general to be triple the export earnings from coffee. This trade is equally important for Jamaica. Cocaine exports from Bolivia far exceed foreign exchange earnings from tin. (With the multiplication of small independent nations in the world, there are now at least a few, e.g. Zaire, where smuggling of normal exports or imports cannot be overlooked as a significant factor in their economies.) In regional and state accounts, the inclusion or exclusion of gambling and prostitution, depending on whether they are legal or illegal, must distort to at least a small degree comparisons of per capita incomes.

The underground economy not only blunts the precision of the national accounts, it also affects the employment and unemployment statistics. The labour force is larger than officially reported by those individuals who get all their income from the underground economy. The Government Accounting Office has estimated these may total as many as 4 – 5 million in the United States. Then, there are many more millions of individuals who get part of their income from this economy. *Fortune* reported on a musician who said: 'I'll work a gig on the books, and when it ends I'll collect unemployment insurance, while that continues, I'll take gigs off the books, and when the unemployment money runs out, I'll do another job on the books to qualify again.' A study by the Institute of Labor and Industrial Relations of the University of Michigan and Wayne State University in nine Detroit neighbourhoods in 1975 found that 'underground' sources provided the majority of babysitting, lawn care, exterior and interior painting, panelling and carpenter work, and more than one-third of the cement, electrical wiring and plumbing work for the 284 families studied (Klein, 1978, p. 29).

An interesting new phenomenon in the industrialized countries is the rise of a barter sector — largely outside the national accounts. It is almost certainly equivalent to less than 1 per cent of GNP but is another element dulling the precision of the accounts. Barter has gone so far that it has become institutionalized in the form of well-organized barter clubs made up of individuals and small businesses willing to swap goods and services. Most clubs use a system of debits and credits, some even issue scrip or 'bartercards' like credit cards and offer a wide range of goods and services. There were in 1981 at least three major chains with franchises across the USA. One company operates internationally with offices in the United Kingdom, Canada and Australia. One particular aspect of the barter section has been called the 'social economy' by Martin D. Lowenthal. This comprises the services of economic value that friends and relatives perform for each other without charge: some families get along quite well on little income as conventionally measured because they use services from both the 'underground' and 'social' economies, while others on the same income are 'truly poor' (Klein, p. 29).

The foregoing discussion has indicated that the estimates for sectors that cover close to half of the GNP in industrialized nations are not precisely accurate and that this seems to be inherent in the nature of these sectors. And, remember, these sectors have been a growing proportion of the total GNP in all industrialized countries. In addition, we have mentioned several sets of activities that are mostly or wholly outside the national accounts all together and yet are significant in the national economy.

Less developed countries

In addition to the problems of measurement and definition of the national accounts that apply to *all countries*, conventional national accounts can capture only very roughly the economies of the *less developed countries*: (1) the accounts are monistic, that is, they consider the whole nation to be sufficiently homogeneous to be treated as a single unit — this assumption is untrue in dualistic economies or economies with important enclave sectors; (2) the accounts are designed for countries that are economically independent, and the accounts of companies under foreign control are not separately presented; (3) expenditure on durable capital goods is considered as 'investment' whether on machinery or 'white elephant' prestige projects, whereas expenditures that may result in the future flow of output, such as on education or nutrition of children, is 'consumption'; (4) non-marketed production is treated cursorily, and own production of villages (e.g. religious, military, and medical services provided on the basis of customary obligation or barter) is completely neglected; (5) it is assumed that reliable statistics do in fact exist on economic activities. This assumption is especially doubtful in the cases of trade, services and traditional self-production. For example, estimates of food output are often derived from some old and unreliable census; output per head is assumed to remain constant with increases in rural population; output prices are assumed to move in line with urban market prices; and very crude assumptions are made about input prices and quantities (Seers, 1976, p. 198). There are similar problems with imputed rent on owner-occupied houses, value of dwelling construction (for Nigeria in 1950, Okigbo estimated 570,000 huts were built while Prest and Stewart's estimate was 2,940,000), peasant capital formation, etc.

The national accounts tend to have an upward bias since the faster-growing industrial activities are overweighted simply because they are more visible and easier to measure. In brief, as Dudley Seers concluded, there is a degree of fantasy in most national accounts of the less developed countries: any competent statistician could easily justify doubling or halving many items (Seers, 1976, p. 200).

Criticism of the accuracy of national accounts data by Morgenstern (1963) was shrugged off by the comment that '. . . the estimates *are* subject to the same general biases from year to year, and the errors to be expected in the change figures are less than those in the absolute figures. No one really cares what the error in the absolute magnitude of the gross national product is, because no one has yet thought up a way to use this figure in isolation' (N. Ruggles, 1964, p. 447; emphasis in original). This is consoling but not convincing. It is the more imprecisely measured parts of the national economy in industrialized countries that seem to be more dynamic than the sectors that can be more precisely measured. In contrast, in less developed countries with large subsistence sectors, over time the growth of the more easily measurable sectors may on balance reduce the present very large margins of fuzziness. Total GNP and per capita GNP figures are widely used for comparisons among countries and over time. The size of GNP per capita may determine, for example, whether a less developed country is eligible to receive economic aid as grants or soft loans or can only borrow on hard terms from the international financial institutions. It does matter then whether people realize how rough the absolute magnitude of gross national product is.

World Development Indicators, published annually by the World Bank, is probably the best single source of data on the economic position of the less developed countries. Between the publication of the *Indicators* for 1978 and the one for 1979, owing to revision of population and national accounts estimates, the figures for GNP per capita and its real growth changed drastically for many countries: Guinea's population decreased from 5.7 million to 5.0 million; per capita GNP went up by 47 per cent from

$150 to $220; the per capita annual real growth rate since 1960 more than tripled. For the low-income countries as a whole, the 1978 volume reported *0.9 per cent* as the average annual growth rate of real GNP per capita over the period 1960 – 76. The 1979 volume gave a figure of *1.4 per cent* for the slightly longer period, 1960 – 77, that is, an increase in the rate of 57 per cent. The precision of these figures is impressive but spurious. The underlying data, as has been pointed out, are far from accurate. Realistically, it is doubtful if GNP or population figures are significant beyond the first or second digit, and certainly not to the first decimal. Had the growth rate been shown to one significant digit, the rate for 1960 – 76 would have been 1 per cent (instead of 0.9) as would the rate for 1960 – 77 (instead of 1.4). The meaningless bouncing around of this rate would have been avoided and truer communication would have resulted.

International comparisons of real national product

For about as long as countries have attempted to calculate national accounts, international comparisons of total and per capita national incomes (or product) have been attempted. For our purposes, there is no need to review this literature here. There are several aspects of this subject that are pertinent, however.

First, in spite of all the theoretical and real difficulties of making inter-spatial (and inter-temporal) comparisons of national product, there is a clear policy and operational need for them. Governments need to have some idea of how one economy compares with others: to get some ideas as to the likely structure or possible pattern of their own development; to secure a basis for burden-sharing exercises (in paying UN costs, in setting quotas, and capital subscriptions and contributions in international agencies); to have some guidance in allocating economic aid to countries, etc. Economists, both as theorists and as policy advisers, need to be able to classify and rank countries in this way, however roughly, and to get some perception of relative rates of change among countries.

Second, on the whole, economists in this field have usually recognized from the very beginning the impossibility of deriving unquestionable precise measures of comparison.

Finally, there has developed a fairly wide consensus that the best feasible means of comparison is through the calculation of purchasing power parities. It is true that the most widely used system is still (1983) that based on conversion of national product statistics of countries through the exchange rate into a common numeraire, usually the US dollar. However, no one, including the World Bank, whose *Atlas* is usually regarded as the standard reference by governments for this purpose, regards the foreign exchange rate conversions as being anything more than the currently available second-best or inferior good. As the director of the World Bank's Economics Department, I was responsible for the creation of the *Atlas*. It is because of the consciousness of the drawbacks of the figures presented that we made a major financial contribution to the United Nations Project for the calculation of purchasing power comparisons. It will be recalled that the drawbacks of a straight foreign exchange rate conversion of national accounts for conversion purposes are, briefly: foreign exchange rates are affected by only a part of total GDP, that is, by prices of goods and services that enter international trade, by transport costs, by the system of protection, by capital flows; a large and varying part of GDP does not enter international trade and is only remotely, if at all, affected by the exchange rate; as between countries, prices of those commodities and services that do not enter international trade tend to be considerably lower in a less developed country than in an industrialized country (e.g. food consumed at home, servants' services, haircuts) and, consequently, the national product of a less developed country is understated in a comparison.

The purchasing power comparison system, most economists in the field now agree, gives a better approximation of the real differences among country national products. This is done by comparing the relative products of two countries in real terms through valuing the quantities of goods and services produced in each country by the same set of prices. Usually a binary comparison is made by first valuing the goods and services of countries A and B (Q_A, Q_B) by A's price weights (P_A) and then by B's price weights (P_B).

$$\frac{P_A Q_A}{P_A Q_B} \quad \text{and} \quad \frac{P_B Q_A}{P_B Q_B}$$

This is essentially the same process as constructing an index number or comparing the changes in the real national product of a single country over time. And, of course, this approach therefore runs into the familiar index number dilemma (mentioned above in chapter 4). That is, the results are different depending upon which price weights are used and there is no logical reason for preferring one to the other. In this case, the relation between the national products of Country A and Country B differs depending upon whether the quantities of product produced in each country are valued at Country A's prices or Country B's prices. For example, for 1970, per capita GDP for the United Kingdom was calculated at 66 per cent of the US per capita GDP using British price weights and at 78 per cent using American weights (Kravis *et al*, 1975, p. 11; and at 53 per cent by the Bank *Atlas*'s foreign exchange rate conversion method).

As in the example, it is to be expected that this method of comparison will always result in Country A's real income appearing higher if Country B's price weights are used. This is because in any comparison of two countries, Country A will tend to consume more of the products that are relatively cheaper in A and less of goods that are dearer in A but cheaper in B. What is important for our purposes here is to note that in these binary comparisons there is no scientific basis to prefer the use of the price weights of A over B or vice versa. Both are equally correct though the answers they give differ. To facilitate comparison through having a single number to use, the two results are often combined by calculating the so-called 'ideal' index, that is, the geometric mean (which is less affected by extremes than the common arithmetic average) of the two.

$$\left(\frac{P_A Q_A}{P_A Q_B} \times \frac{P_B Q_A}{P_B Q_B} \right)^{1/2}$$

In the UK example cited above, the ideal index would show British per capita GDP as being 72 per cent of that of the US. However, even though this ideal index may be used, it is only a proxy for the more realistic spread between the two binary competition numbers.

The calculations of the binary comparisons entail making arbitrary decisions in the classification of the commodites and services between the two countries to which a common set of prices is going to be applied. This point is perhaps best made by citing Usher's example of a comparison between Thailand and the United Kingdom. He took a limited number of commodities and showed how the results could be made to vary widely depending upon how finely the commodities were specified. If the commodities were specified as mangoes, apples, buffalo meat, beef, rice flour, wheat flour, for example, the application of British price weights exaggerates the comparative Thai standard of living. The result was to show an income for Thailand 20 times higher than that of the United Kingdom on British price weights, and 10 per cent of the UK on Thai price weights. On the other hand, if the commodities were thrown into very broad classes ('fruit', 'meat', 'flour') you could show Thai income equal to the British (Usher, 1968, pp. 24 – 6).

In addition to this imprecision and all the other elements of imprecision in the calculation of individual country national accounts that have been discussed earlier in this chapter, there are some other factors that come into play in the calculation of the comparison of national products. It is intuitively obvious that the closer the two countries being compared are in their social systems, levels of development and patterns of values, tastes and consumption, the more precise these comparisons are in relation to reality. The farther apart the two countries are in these respects, the less precise the comparison can be. In comparing France and Germany in 1970, for example, figures showing that they had roughly equivalent per capita GDP's could be regarded with considerable confidence as properly representing reality. But in comparing the United States and India, about all that one could say with assurance is that the US per capita GDP was a multiple of that of India, and perhaps in the range of 10 – 20 times higher.

Relation of GNP to measurement of welfare

The premise underlying the collection and calculation of national accounts estimates is that the flow of material goods and services they measure has a relationship to individual and societal welfare. Personal income is fundamentally only a means to attain well-being — an input into rather than a measure of individual well-being. It can be shown that national income is a proxy of well-being under a set of narrow unrealistic assumptions (the economy is closed, all production takes one period with no carry-over, all consumers are identical and incomes are equal, technology is given with increasing marginal cost throughout, there is perfect competition among all consumers and producers). In these impossible conditions, prices equal marginal utilities and marginal costs (the price-line that represents the value of production at market prices touches the production-possibility curve and the collective indifference curve at the same point) (Hicks, 1981, particularly Essay 9). However, once these assumptions are modified, as of course they must be in reality, the national accounts become very imperfect proxies for welfare.

The higher the per capita GNP of an industrialized country, the more it may include items that do not contribute to individual welfare. In the business sector of the economy, it is recognized that some goods are intermediate commodities. That is, some commodities are inputs for the final commodities produced and are not a part of final output; e.g. flour produced for the making of bread, which is the final commodity. But some consumer expenditures are also for inputs or intermediate goods and services even though present national accounting conventions treat them as final output. Kuznets, a founder of national accounting, has pointed out that as the result of economic growth the pattern of life imposed on groups in the population, as a condition of participation in the economy, imposes costs on them that they must meet; e.g. costs of commuting. Consumer expenditures on these costs should therefore be excluded from gross output. Kuznets estimates that in the United States in the 1950s excluding such items would have reduced GNP as conventionally measured by over 20 per cent (Kuznets, 1966, p. 227).

In recent years, we have become aware of still another problem from economic growth that affects measurement of national output and its relationship to welfare. When the growth of industries pollutes the atmosphere, destroys rivers and lakes and turns the environment into an abomination to the sight, this mostly or entirely does not enter into the national accounts calculus. But when 'defensive' goods or 'anti-bads' in the form of expenditures on anti-pollution measures are produced, these are considered costs and are a charge against final output. The improvements in good health, in a cleaner, safer, more attractive environment and, consequently, in greater enjoyment of life that can result from such expenditures are not directly measured and are not counted in the total product.

There is an even more far-reaching analysis by Fred Hirsch (1976) that gives additional reasons why the welfare significance of the national accounts changes in the process of economic growth. It explains why in more developed countries a given increase in per capita incomes appears to add little to perceived individual welfare. Briefly, Hirsch shows that there are two kinds of economic goods: 'material' and 'positional'.

'Material' goods in his definition are those commodities and services whose enjoyment by an individual is independent of the number of other people who are consuming them. The fact that other people have good waterproof boots does not keep me from enjoying mine. My appreciation of a good meal does not lessen because other people are also satisfactorily feeding themselves. We all improve our standard of living when each of us eats better. In poor countries, as economic growth assures more and more people of provision of the basic physiological necessities of food, clothing, shelter, an increase in GNP is associated with an increase in total welfare.

The distinguishing characteristic of 'positional goods' is that they are commodities and services where individual enjoyment of a particular good is affected by how many others also possess it. The more car-ownership spreads, the more the resulting congestion reduces the pleasure and the transportation services an individual car provides. As people's incomes rise, they discover that the very fact that they and many others can now afford to visit a desirable tourist area ruins the place. The household and personal servants the affluent used to enjoy are no longer affordable as the number of affluent increases. What the wealthy have today can no longer be afforded by the rest of us tomorrow as we attain the level of income the rich used to have. The desirable jobs that a secondary school graduate used to be able to get now require a college degree since nearly everybody today has completed secondary school.

Once a country has, like the industrialized countries today, gone well beyond the point where the basic physiological necessities are assured to the mass of the population, expenditures on positional goods are important to an increasing proportion of the population. An individual's welfare and happiness, insofar as they are related to his possession of economic goods, are therefore increasingly importantly related to his *relative* income — this income compared to that of others — rather than the absolute level.

This explains the 'Easterlin paradox'. In surveying the available data on a number of countries, Easterlin (1974) found that people in high per capita income countries did not appear to be happier than people in low per capita countries. He also found that in the United States, although per capita incomes have risen substantially since World War II, people did not appear to have become happier. At any one time in a country, however, the higher the income the more likely was the individual to consider himself happier than someone of lower income. If happiness can be considered to be related to 'welfare', then welfare does not appear to go up as GNP goes up. A country with a pleasant climate, with healthy, well-fed people and with a culture of simple pleasures may have a lower per capita GNP than a country with a bad climate, a big defence industry and a culture that promotes individual misery. The people of the former, though 'poorer', are much better off than the people of the latter.

In sum, the national accounts are not a precise measure of the physical quality of life, welfare or happiness. This does not mean, however, that national accounts are useless. That 'riches do not happiness bring' is undoubtedly true in the sense that 'riches' are not a necessary and sufficient condition for 'happiness'. However, it is also true that with greater material means you have more options: you can still make yourself miserable but you can also get commodities and services you want, you have more openings for self-expression and you can avoid material deprivations and miseries you do not want. Similarly, with all the difficulties there are in measuring national product, and the very loose relationship between national product and welfare, the quantity of goods and services available to a nation *is* of significant importance for the range of choice the nation has available to it.

The national accounts are merely an accounting system. Accounting systems measure only what they are able to measure. The national accounts do present a more or less accurate map of the economy and its interconnections and do give a rough measure of current changes in it. Problems arise when people read into the accounts value significances and relationships to behaviour in reality that they do not have. As long as one remains fully aware of what the accounting system is measuring and what it is not, even the present national accounting systems can be useful tools.

This chapter has covered only a part of the weaknesses in the present system of national accounts from the standpoint of analytical relevance and appropriate boundaries. As Reynolds has remarked, we need constantly to re-examine our measurement systems to avoid pseudo-precision: 'Many of the conventions of the system of national accounts, such as the definition of capital and capital services, the meaning of final output, and the valuation of government production are debatable, and . . . a shift to different concepts would make a large difference in the results' (Reynolds, 1971, p. 324). Among other criticisms raised in the literature are, for example: the absence of a distinction between capital and current accounts in the household and government sectors; the treatment of work as being a complete 'bad' and leisure as a complete 'good'; the inadequate attention to the investment aspect compared to current consumption of the expenditures on health and education; the exclusion of value-added in the household sector. However, to modify the system to meet these criticisms would entail moving from accounts that are based on recorded transactions and more sharply defined to accounts that would generally be based more on estimation, imputation and much less precisely defined. If progress is to be made towards constructing a system of accounts that will provide a better proxy measure of individual and societal well-being, this is the direction that work will have to go (see, in particular, the important proposal by Juster, Courant and Dow, 1981). The more accurately we want the national accounts to grasp this aspect of reality, the rougher and more imprecise they will have to be.

6

Balance of Payments

> . . . no kind of ignorance can be more dangerous than ignorance
> regarding the limits and limitations of one's knowledge.
>
> T. W. Hutchison, *Knowledge and Ignorance in Economics*

In the last chapter we focused on the national income and product
measures of the aggregate economy, which are at the centre of most
macroeconomics in the analysis of the economy of a country. No
country, however, can afford the luxury of ignoring other
countries and its balance of payments, which attempts to measure
the flow of transactions between it and the rest of the world. The
balance of payments covers movements of capital or financial
assets in and out of a country and its international trade in services
and in goods. The question we consider in this chapter is: how
precisely accurate can the balance of payments accounts be? First,
comprehensive statistics on capital movements among countries do
not exist. The statistics that are available are notoriously inaccurate. The size and variability of the discrepancy between estimated
annual capital inflows and outflows among countries, as well as its
sign, make the available figures a rather insecure basis for
conclusions about what is happening to world capital flows
(J. S. Smith, 1966, p. 20). This unreliability is not due solely to inadequate reporting by the less developed countries: an NBER study
found that coverage of capital transactions by continental
European industrialized countries was not better than that of the
LDCs (Michael, 1971).

Comprehensive statistics are, however, gathered or estimated on
the balance of payments on current account of practically all
countries in the world. Since every export or sale of a commodity

or service from one country is also an import or purchase by some other country, the net sum in each category of the current accounts of all the countries of the world should be zero. In practice, this sub-account balancing cannot take place since countries may have or apply different definitions to the same transaction (processing of goods may be in the merchandise account or services account, what may be a government item on the payment side may be in the private sector on the receipts side, etc.). But the overall accounts of the whole world should in theory net out to zero. In actual fact, this is also too much to expect since it is reasonable that some differences in efficiency and coverage would exist among statistical offices in the different countries of the world. Until fairly recently, the net discrepancy proved to be fairly small — $0.1 billion in 1969, for instance.

Since 1970, the yearly current account discrepancy has grown rapidly. By 1980, the global net sum of the current account balances of payments of the countries of the world showed a net yearly negative discrepancy of $36 billion. What this means is that the true current account balances of some or even most countries were either in greater surplus or smaller deficit in varying degrees than their official figures indicated. This overall discrepancy was the net result of a global deficit on invisible account (services, investment income, transfers) of $75 billion partly offset by a global export surplus of $39 billion. The invisibles discrepancy was equivalent to 9 per cent of recorded world invisibles payments while the trade discrepancy was 2 per cent of recorded world exports.

The OECD, with the help of the balance of payments experts of the OECD countries, the International Monetary Fund and the World Bank, carried out a special study in 1982 to attempt to identify the main causes of this growing and worrying discrepancy in the accounts (OECD, 1982b). Among the most significant factors that might be involved, the OECD study suggested, are the following. In trade, the net balance, which is persistently positive, appears to be partly due to time lag. Goods leaving Europe, for example, are recorded as exports when the ship leaves but are recorded as imports only when the ship arrives in Latin America. With rising prices and growing trade, this can be a continuous cause of discrepancy. Another cause appears to be the export of ships to open-registry countries. When Korea sells a ship to an oil company for Liberian registry, it appears as a Korean export, but it does not appear at the other end as a Liberian import or indeed as the import of any country. Smuggling of goods into some countries may also explain how goods are shown in the statistics as leaving one country but are never shown as arriving in another. In the invisibles account, where the discrepancy is larger and negative, apparently countries tend to under-report their receipts in most categories of this account. One of the factors here is the channelling of receipts such as investment income through international tax havens such as Panama where they are often not recorded. Existing recording methods often have difficulties in getting data on receipts of payments for services such as construction, engineering and consultancy. There is a particularly large discrepancy in the figures for official transfers in the form of development aid. Compared to the figures of the donor governments, the recipient government figures miss about 40 per cent of the aid total. There may also be overestimation of the expenditures on some of the other items such as payments for transportation.

If this sketch of some of the problems is not sufficiently convincing to induce caution in using balance of payments statistics, the OECD study warns in passing that while countries have gradually been applying the concepts and definitions of the standard balance of payments manual of the International Monetary Fund (1977), they are doing so mostly for current reporting without going back to revise the historical series.

In most countries, it is generally felt, and correctly so, that trade statistics are among the most reliable of the economic data available. Unfortunately, this is more a reflection on the poor quality of the other statistics than a compliment to the trade data. What many economists do not realize is that the most figures on trade flows are far from precisely accurate. This is aside from the normal incidence of human errors: at the end of the 1960s it was discovered that the British statistics had consistently understated British exports for nearly six years! A basic paper by Luc DeWulf of the International Monetary Fund (1978) is most revealing in this regard.

In most countries trade statistics are compiled from customs data. This means, first, that they are dependent on the customs declarations of importers. Most import taxes are *ad valorem*. Consequently, given the *ad valorem* rate, the range between the invoice price and the real import price depends on the risk of being detected by the customs authorities, on the penalties levied if detected, and on the standard of ethics practised in the society. If there is also the possibility of corruption of customs officials, there is little probability that there is a fixed unchanging relationship between real price and declared price. Second, customs valuation practices and customs duties are to some extent interchangeable policy instruments: fiscal and trade objectives can be achieved through the manipulation of either one or both. (a) If a country raises its customs duties, this does not directly affect the accuracy of its trade statistics (except through the incentive factor mentioned above). (b) If a country raises the valuations applied to its imports, it may achieve the same revenue or trade results as in (a), but it also distorts its trade statistics. An adequate valuation system often requires the investigation of trade between related parties and may depend on the quality of the bookkeeping of the importer. Quite obviously, in much of the world, the demands of an adequate valuation system exceed local customs capabilities.

One cannot assume that any deviation between the price declared to customs and the real invoice price is always an understatement. If the country has exchange control and there is a black market rate of exchange, depending on the spread between the official rate and the black market rate contrasted to the size of the *ad valorem* tariff rate, the importer may have an incentive to overdeclare or underdeclare the value of his imports. Moreover, the results of this calculation will vary from time to time depending on the relative changes in these two margins (as well as on the severity and efficiency of the customs and foreign exchange control enforcement efforts).

In a country having foreign exchange control or export taxes, similar incentives to distort export statistics also operate. In a recent extreme case, the value of coffee exports from Zaire was shown in the trade statistics as 80 million Zaires (or around $100 million equivalent) in 1976; an independent estimate, taking into account the explosion in coffee prices that had taken place, was that the true value was closer to 272 million Zaires (or over $300 million equivalent) (Young, 1978, p. 174).

The preference given by many countries to capital goods imports under foreign exchange controls and the fact that there is no well-organized market for these goods with standard price quotations make it difficult to control over-invoicing of these goods. This distorts not only the trade statistics but also the investment and national accounts of the importing country since often the estimate of the investment component of GNP is based on the value of imported capital goods. As a result of these factors, an administrative decision may have considerable impact on statistics of crucial sectors without any real change having occurred at all: for example, if a government removes capital export controls, its reported imports and investment may drop and its commodity exports go up while the real value of its trade may not change at all.

The growth of multinational corporations has increased the possibility of distortion in the trade statistics. It has been estimated by Paul Streeten that around one-quarter to one-third of world trade in manufactures is intra-firm trade and, therefore, not at arm's length. This proportion may be even larger for LDCs (Streeten, 1973, p. 6). More than half of all US imports consist of US intra-firm transactions (Helleiner, 1981, p. 11). The transfer prices that different parts of a multinational corporation will use to invoice trade with one another will be influenced by the different tax rates on profits in the countries concerned, their tariffs, restrictions on profit remittances, exchange rate risks, differential inflation rates, and the different social and political risks involved. With the world as it is, transfer prices that differ from free market prices will often be profitable and, hence, likely to be applied. Since these transfer prices affect not only trade statistics but also the country where the corporation decides to show its profits, the US Internal Revenue Service has been increasingly concerned in recent years about the transfer price policies of US multinational corporations. An illustration of this also shows how the trade statistics get distorted in the process. A US pharmaceutical company exports to its subsidiary in a low-tax less developed country some empty bottles, a drug in powder form and some empty capsules. The subsidiary assembles and ships the bottle of drugs in capsules back to the United States. The US company charges its subsidiary $1 for the subsidiary's imports of the materials needed to produce one bottle and pays the subsidiary $8 per bottle exported to the United States. The US company then sells the drug at a little more or even a little less than $8. The subsidiary thus has a profit of $7 less a minimal amount of labour cost; the US company shows no profit or even a loss. Thus the trade statistics are distorted, US taxes avoided and the less developed country's feelings of being exploited are further aggravated.

Another source of discrepancy in the trade accounts is the valuation of official governmental donations. Donor countries typically show the value of these goods at higher prices than may be recorded by the recipient countries. The very existence of aid or loan tying implies that the price of the goods concerned in the donor country is likely to be above the world export price.

There have been all too few actual case studies directed to estimating how imprecise trade data actually are. An interesting study by Seiji Naya and Theodore Morgan on the Southeast Asian countries, comparing the reciprocal import and export data for several years on trade among these countries and with countries elsewhere, found large discrepancies to be the norm even after allowing for an arbitrary 10 per cent margin for transport costs. Compared to the arbitrary expected ratio of 1.10 (import valuation declared at the recipient country over the export valuation declared by the country of origin), the ratios were 0.46 for Singapore; 1.14 for Thailand; 1.34, Philippines; 1.4, Burma; 1.44, Ceylon; 2.11, Malaya; and 10.47 for Indonesia! (Naya and Morgan, 1974, p. 127). The authors explain that the discrepancies might be caused by transport costs, different recording definitions used by different countries, simple errors in counting and recording, smuggling, bribes to customs officers to falsify the records, and understatement or overstatement of values to conceal capital flight. The authors conclude that errors in trade data frequently are substantial and can be overwhelmingly large. For some countries, the best guess of an informed and conscientious student can be more accurate than the official figures.

As the above discussion indicates, the forces that result in distorted trade statistics tend to be strongest in less developed countries. At the same time, even if accurate statistics were available, institutional changes, sharp changes in import-substituting capacity and the impact on national product from the severe variations of the tropical climates (where most less developed countries are located) all mean that no stable lasting relationship can be expected to hold between GNP and imports. If statistics do show a constant relationship, it may be due to collinearity — that is, because the capital formation estimates in the GNP are directly based on statistics of capital goods imports. Consequently, it is highly probable that a calculated 'propensity to import' for many less developed countries is purely an *ex post* relationship and not a real propensity at all.

7

Macroeconomic Models

> Economics is a science of thinking in terms of models joined to the art of choosing models which are relevant to the contemporary world, . . . Good economists are scarce because the gift . . . to choose good models . . . appears to be a very rare one.
>
> John Maynard Keynes, *The Collected Writings*, vol.XIV

There are various theories about what economics is. For our purposes here, we can accept that economics has two main functions: to explain (or clarify) existing or past economic reality, and to predict future economic events. (And, consequently, armed with this knowledge we can, in some measure, control or influence effectively some aspects of economic reality.) In this respect, whether we use mathematical-language or word-language does not matter so long as there is adequate communication. Mathematics has an advantage in being inherently more rigorous if used correctly and more efficient in conveying some meanings and in applying logic. Word-language has an advantage in having a much richer vocabulary and in being less susceptible to irrelevancy: mathematical economics tempts the economist to believe that it is sufficient that a model be good mathematics (internally consistent) and to disregard whether it also be good economics (empirically correct, i.e. externally consistent or isomorphic with the real world).

As we have seen in chapter 2, in moving from purely symbolic mathematical theory to numerical statements applicable to the real world, errors are inevitable. In economics *per se*, additional elements of inaccuracy and imprecision are inevitable (see chapters 3 and 4). Economics deals with people who are not passive but react to new information and events — most of which are non-recurring. The data come from sources that have an interest in the information provided and the interest may not be that the information is accurate. There is limited scope for experimentation to check theories. The whole structure of economic reality is in flux — parameters are unstable, lags differ and vary. External events with major impact on the structure are uncontrollable and often unpredictable. The individual units are indefinite and classes inexact, consequently empirical concepts are 'loose' — have no sharp boundaries but shade imperceptibly into their opposites. It has been impossible so far to quantify exactly some important elements of the economic structure.

As an economic model tries to cover a wide sector of the economy or the whole economy, it becomes increasingly vulnerable to what might be called 'political – economic' errors. With the growing role of government in the economy, economic issues have become increasingly political issues. As a result, many corporations, unions and professional bodies have learned that they can achieve profits or other benefits as easily by government actions as by their own efforts in the marketplace. In a pluralistic society like that of the advanced industrial nations there is a substantial interpenetration of the government organs of control, corporations and other pressure groups. This has been popularly recognized to be true in the extreme case of Japan where the position is even summarized in the catch-words 'Japan, Inc.' The situation is not very different in France and Italy. In all the industrial countries, economic organizations violate the silent assumption of economic theory and seek to influence political organizations in pursuit of their own ends. What this means is that the very structure of an important equation in a macroeconomic model may be changed overnight by an industry calling in the political power to rectify or to distort the previous relationships.

In applying economic theory to reality in the form of a model (i.e. a set of structural equations), the degree of precision built into the model will of course vary with the particular instance. The thrust of the argument in this book is that the optimum precision attainable depends upon the margins of error in the data to be used and in the knowledge and the sharpness of the concepts embodied in the parameters. More sophistication or more refinement in the model are not necessarily better if the data are not very accurate and the concepts are loose.

This chapter tries to bring out some of the limitations in the construction and use of macroeconomic models; it is not an argument against such models *per se*. It must be recognized that econometrics, in general, represented a major step forward in economics through its attempts to measure and to quantify economic concepts and relationships. The criticisms in the preceding chapters are of the application of econometric techniques with insufficient appreciation of the limitations flowing out of the nature of economic reality. Economic models are useful tools in confronting reality in the attempt to understand and to influence it. Criticism is justifiable not of the tool but of its use without an adequate understanding of its limitations.

The impact of all the elements of imprecision in economics is greatest in models that attempt to grasp a whole economy and to predict the course of economic events. (The standard approach to building such models appears to be the assumption that a true model of the structure of reality can be produced of correctly specified equations with stable parameters and a white noise error process.) In spite of a few stochastic elements built into the equations, these models are basically mechanical behaviour models. They must assume behaviour that is 'necessary' or 'invariant' rather than voluntary in some sense. They have to assume that the concepts, relationships and structure of the past will remain constant in the future or will change in some regular, predictable way. They have to assume that the multitude of exogenous factors either net out or have the same impact as in the past or again are largely predictable. In fact, even the regularity of seasonal factors is becoming less important — while all economies are still subject to the regular procession of the seasons, economies like the British and American, where agriculture is now under 5 per cent of GNP, are clearly less influenced by seasonal factors than decades ago when agriculture's share was several times larger. The increasing role of the state in the mixed and socialist economies and the larger role played by the latter in world trade also make prediction based on purely economic models more difficult. It would indeed be surprising, therefore, if such macroeconomic models did succeed in correctly predicting major changes in the economy that were not obvious to anyone with informed common sense. And, in fact, the record of performance substantiates this scepticism.

T. C. Koopmans, among the most noted of econometricians, in reviewing the experience to 1957, states: 'We must face the fact that models using elaborate theoretical and statistical tools and concepts have not done decisively better, in the majority of available tests, than the most simple-minded and mechanical extrapolation formulae' (Koopmans, 1957, p. 212). The experience since then with macroeconomic models has not been any better. In 1973, in analysing the results of a conference (co-sponsored by the US National Bureau of Economic Research and the Committee on Economic Stabilization of the Social Science Research Council) to explore applications of econometric models to the analysis of business cycles, Karl Brunner found that, while the levels of 'subtle sophistication' were quite high, the performance of the models unfortunately showed an unimpressive forecasting record. In more than 50 per cent of the series examined, 'naive' models outperformed the econometric models. Even the best econometric model exceeded the naive models and all other models at most in 20 per cent of the series (Brunner, 1973, p. 929). Brunner also went on to criticize the practice of some econometricians of manipulating the available numbers without regard to what the numbers or relationships are supposed to mean. One should not use numbers without analytical or empirical justification. In the absence of justification, one is engaged in a meaningless numerological exercise and speaking nonsense.

Every six months, the Organization for Economic Co-operation and Development (OECD) prepares seasonally adjusted forecasts for the forthcoming half-year of the gross national product, the implicit price deflator of GNP and the balance of trade for the seven major OECD countries (Canada, France, Germany, Italy, Japan, the United Kingdom and the United States). Smyth and Ash, in a statistical study of these forecasts compared to simple projections, conclude that the OECD forecasts are in no way superior and that the accuracy of the forecasts shows no significant improvement over time (Smyth and Ash, 1975, pp. 363 – 4).

At the American Economic Association meeting in 1977, a session was devoted to an evaluation of forecasts of the US GNP. One of the conclusions from the session was that the most 'refined' or 'sophisticated' models do not forecast better than the individuals who make back-of-the envelope informal forecasts. The most important finding of the meeting however, was, that, while the forecasts normally did do better than pure mechanical extrapolation, they did poorly in the really important test, that of forecasting turning points in the cycle. When real GNP turned down in 1954, 1958, 1970 and 1974, eight of ten predictions for these years forecast continued rises. The year 1974 was the beginning of the most serious recession since the 1930s but '. . . forecasters across the field missed it' (Zarnowitz, 1978, pp. 316 – 17).

It is helpful to have the empirical evidence that forecasts from macroeconomic models are not exact, but this result is to be expected from the discussion in chapters 3 and 4 above. The parameters in these models are basically established from the statistical record of the past. But, with an economic structure that is continually changing, in calculating these parameters we are analysing an economic structure that no longer exists. Even key variables that remain the same never quite interact in the same way each time because the circumstances differ, the strength of the economic forces at work vary, and especially the time for a given effect to show itself varies. The exogenous factors affecting the economy are bound to be different: we may try to force the economy into a procrustean bed of econometric equations, but we delude ourselves if we think it will remain there (Cairncross, 1969, p. 800).

The econometric models of the US economy have grown ever larger. The models designed by Lawrence Klein in the 1940s had 12 equations; the three main models in 1980 have over 400, over 600 and around 800 equations, respectively. While these models have become increasingly complex and sophisticated, it has also become clear that they do not serve the function that truly scientific models do. In the natural sciences, the very essence of a model is that it is unambiguously defined so that tests of conformity with the real world can be carried out by anyone and the same answers secured to the same degree of accuracy (Zinman, 1978, p. 31). In these econometric macro-models, in contrast, the operators use a procedure that is usually called 'fine-tuning' (but is also labelled 'fudging' by some irreverent modelling types). Fine-tuning consists of the operator looking at the initial results generated by his model and, if he decides they are not reasonable, he then reaches into his model to change constant term values in his behavioural equations or the exogenous variables and so makes the results come out consistent with his judgement. What comes out is essentially a forecast by the econometrician based on his subjective, internal model rather than a forecast by the explicit model. Consequently, different people can derive different results from the same explicit model for the same set of objective data.

There is nothing intrinsically wrong with this procedure as long as it is clearly and fully exposed. On the contrary, it recognizes correctly the inherent complexity and flux of the economy and the necessity, as a result, of using judgement based on a wide and rich experience in making economic predictions. In celestial mechanics, one would lose confidence in the planned course of a planetary probe if one became aware that the results of the equations were 'corrected' by someone's judgement. In economics, one should lose confidence in the predictions of an economist if we are told that they represent the exact results cranked out of his uncorrected model. What is questionable is whether this whole complicated 'scientific' array of hundreds of equations is not needlessly costly since it has not improved the prediction record over vastly simpler models. It is hardly a sufficient justification that, in our scientific age, economic forecasts may be more believable if they appear to be the outcome of a highly complicated computerized model.

A second set of macroeconomic models, which has had widespread attention, is the long-term economic growth models, particularly in the less developed countries. In the industrial countries, these models are no longer the fad and are being rapidly forgotten. It does not take much experience, for example, to conclude that any explanation of Japanese economic growth is grossly inadequate that focuses on capital – output ratios and the like and omits the high emphasis that Japanese culture places on intellectual achievement and team effort. In the less developed countries, lip service at least is still paid to them in the belief that somehow or other they should be helpful for the framing of economic policy even though in practice it proves impossible to make use of them.

The models that have been constructed for less developed countries are subject to all the difficulties of precision that have been discussed in earlier chapters. The attempt to secure even reasonably accurate data from and through people who are often at best semi-literate is enormous. To the degree that economic development is proceeding, erosion in the meaning of concepts and of the parameters established is also taking place. While the concepts of empirical reality are not necessarily looser than in the more developed countries, even less work has been done on them since the temptation and practice is to import economic concepts wholesale from the more developed countries. For example, the distinction or the dividing line between consumption and investment in a less developed country is harder to draw and is even more blurred than in a more industrialized country. In Africa, some mines make a regular practice of feeding miners a proper diet for several weeks after they are recruited from rural areas before assigning them to work below the surface — these consumption expenditures on building the strength of human capital result in a higher increment to output than equivalent expenditures on added equipment.

The formal growth models usually focus on investment expenditure, the supply of capital goods and the volume of imports. The tacit assumption is that expenditure on capital goods is equivalent to investment, whereas in less developed countries expenditure that leads to greater returns in the future covers a much broader category, for example eradication of a debilitating disease, training in skills (see chapter 10). In a country with exchange controls, expenditure on an imported machine is often merely a way of disguising capital flight (i.e. the importer remits a larger sum than the machine is worth to the supplier as a pass-through to a foreign bank account).

In less developed countries, changes in major social and personal determinants — openness to acceptance of proven innovations such as improved seeds, the effectiveness and honesty of a bureaucracy, geographical and occupational mobility, attitudes to work and savings, the volume and receptivity to external contact — may be decisive factors in the pace of economic development. Macroeconomic models cannot predict such changes accurately.

Arun Shourie (1972) has made a devastating technical analysis of the highly aggregated macroeconomic regression models of developing countries. In reviewing some 45 models that have been proposed for developing countries, he points out that the underlying data are so bad that many refinements in estimation procedure like multiple least squares are pointless. (The trade statistics are the only data in which most economists place a great deal of confidence, but see chapter 6 above.) Often the high coefficients of determination that are found are due to one series having been estimated from the other. In Colombia, one model-maker discovered a strong relationship between imports of capital goods and investment. A contrary result would have been surprising since in Colombia fixed investment other than construction was estimated by applying multipliers to capital goods imports for that sector.

Shourie shows that the common statistical assumptions are dangerous (i.e. that errors in each variable are independent of the variable, of other variables in the equation and of errors in other variables.) One model projected the savings gap for Kenya to be dominant (i.e. that growth was most hampered by saving falling short of the possibilities of investment) and therefore recommended that the marginal savings rate be raised from the existing 11.3 per cent to 25 per cent; revised national accounts for the same period made nonsense of the recommendation by estimating that the savings rate was already over 25 per cent. The coefficients of a fitted regression equation cannot, as is usually done, be labelled with the names of phenomena in the real world. This is because, in a very large number of cases, the explanatory variables are strongly related to each other, and there is a strong likelihood that the equations are incomplete and some of the excluded variables may be strongly related to the included variables. Just because the particular functional form of equation seems to fit the sample period data well may not mean that the relationship is the correct one for the future. Often several alternative equations fit as well. But the different equations will yield widely divergent projections and, therefore, policy recommendations for the future.

With all these different possibilities in specifying a model, it is quite possible that any resulting projections and policy recommendations are nothing more than a mechanical output of the particular choices made by the model-builder. Much of this, I might comment by the way, is the result of a fairly common fallacy committed by some model-builders. Regression equations are so easy to compute these days that the 'fallacy of affirming a consequent' is very easy to fall into: that is, 'E' is observed to be true, 'E' can be deduced logically from 'D', therefore that hypothesis 'D' must also be true. But 'E' could also be deduced from hypothesis 'A' or 'B' or 'C'. For instance, it is ascertained that $2 million is missing from the US Treasury; it is not legitimate to conclude that Richard Nixon stole it, even though the observation could be fully accounted for by this hypothesis. An alternative hypothesis that it was Spiro Agnew who was the thief could also fully account for the observation.

Finally, even if all of the foregoing were correctible and the 'correct' decisions were always made, there is serious doubt whether regression equations can be used at all for projecting values of variables that, Shourie points out, are very often two to five times beyond the range of values covered by the observations in the sample period. Aside from the flux in structure and concepts mentioned in preceding chapters, the major objective of developing countries is in fact to change the structure of their economies. Using the regression equations implies that the structure of the developing country in the future will be as in the past or that the structural change will be in the same pattern as of the sample period. (There is now quite an extensive literature on the defects in the comprehensive planning models in the less developed countries. Among the best are: Streeten (1972), Chs 5 and 6; Bauer and Walters, 1975; Stolper (1966, 1969); Mason (1958).)

Lester Thurow (1977) has pointed out that econometric models failed as a means of testing whether clearly specified models could be statistically verified by the data. As could be expected from the discussion in chapter 4, it turned out that equations and coefficients were not stable: equations that fitted historic data well proved to be poor predictors of the future. Now, econometric models are used rather to show that particular theories are consistent with the data — but other theories are also consistent with the data. Thurow cites business investment and labour supply functions as examples. Econometric investigations were not able to find the expected theoretical results showing up in their equations, that is, that rising interest rates resulted in less business investment and lower rates in more. So econometric equations were then designed in such a way that interest rates '. . .were mathematically forced to have the right sign. The equations did not test the theory but they described what the world would look like if the theory were correct' (Thurow, 1977, p. 84). In labour supply functions, econometric efforts to measure and identify 'income effects' (with a higher wage, the utility of the marginal dollar drops and the worker is inclined to work *less*) and 'substitution effects' (with a higher wage, the cost of leisure or not-working goes up, and the worker is inclined to work *more*) have failed. As a result, models have given up and make the labour force a function of job availabilities rather than wages. Instead of using labour supply models derived from empirical estimation of the real world, models now start from mathematical representations where work and leisure stand in the 'correct' relationship to each other. These models are then used to calculate the impact of some public policy on labour supply. 'The models are used empirically but they are not empirical validations of the theory at all' (Thurow, 1977, p. 84).

Optimizing models — those designed to guide a decision-maker to make the best economic decision — have proved themselves valuable for some problems at the micro level (plant or firm, sometimes a highly organized sector like power). In these cases, the basic elements, such as input and output prices, technological relations, time preference and the decision rules, can be objectively ascertained and fairly precisely estimated. But as the scope of such models widens towards including the whole economy they become useless, or 'pseudo-optimizing models' as Reynolds has called them (Reynolds, 1971, p. 312).

The foregoing brief remarks on the very large subject of macro-models in economics in economics can serve to indicate only a possible conclusion: that the term 'model' has too precise a meaning for most of the sets of structural equations that we are able to build in economics. 'Model' carries with it the implication of a mechanism that exactly simulates the behaviour of a larger mechanical system or of a blueprint of the essential elements of a larger system. Economics cannot be this exact — and it is misleading to imply that it is. Perhaps we should use the word 'sketch' or (picking up a thought from Kuznets) 'construct' as being more accurately descriptive of what we produce. Finally, since except for very limited subject matter an economic model cannot be considered as even approximating a mechanical model or blueprint, the conclusion follows that an economic model cannot serve as a director of automatic action or for mandating economic decisions — analytical insight through training and experience remains indispensable.

At the economy-wide level, rough models that isolate a few factors and relationships can be helpful in demonstrating the importance of strategic sectors and relationships and in providing guidance in economic and financial policy-making. Leontief input – output models, for example, have a very simple structure and their fundamental building blocks are at best only reasonably good approximations (fixed technology, constant returns to scale, etc.) but, as a consequence, they work well in providing guidance to policy decisions in the short run. Similarly in my experience as a development economist in an operating institution like the World Bank, Kuznets' less precise, less 'refined' analysis has provided much more valuable insight and understanding of the economic development process than the whole mass of highly 'sophisticated' macro-models that are churned out to fill many pages of the economic journals and are as rapidly forgotten (see Georgescu-Roegen, 1971, p. 341, and Tintner, 1966, p. 119).

8

Microeconomics

Nothing is harder for me than to believe in men's consistency, nothing easier than to believe in their inconsistency. . . . All contradictions may be found in me . . . I have nothing to say about myself absolutely, simply and solidly without confusion and without mixture . . .

Montaigne, *Essays*

In this chapter, we shall see how the paradigm of 'loose concepts' applies to two basic elements of microeconomics: the theory of the consumer and the theory of the firm. Both of these depend on individual economic behaviour, which is the foundation on which modern economics is built. On this, as Koopmans points out, we have good sources of knowledge through introspection of ourselves, questioning other individuals through interview or questionnaire, and even small-scale experiments (Koopmans, 1970, p. 150).

Theory of the consumer

The basic postulate of consumer behaviour, on which the theory of value rests, states that each consumer has a complete ordering by preference of all commodity bundles whose consumption is possible to him, and that in given circumstances consumption levels are therefore completely determined. In plain language, what this says is that it is assumed that consumers are rational and selfish: they know which commodities will satisfy them best and they spend their money accordingly. This postulate, Lionel Robbins (1962) maintains, is drawn from our everyday experience and is obvious. A closer examination shows, however, that one cannot be so confident that consumption levels are 'completely determined'. And, in fact, we shall see rather that there is an inherent lack of precision in consumer preference orderings.

Koopmans has pointed out that the postulate does not conform exactly to reality (Koopmans, 1957, pp. 136 – 7). It overlooks the pleasure a consumer may get by randomly varying his consumption pattern. On the other hand, a consumer may decide he prizes the security or comfort he gets by maintaining the same consumption pattern in spite of a change in circumstances — say a drop in income. More generally, the mapping of a consumer's preferences (or indifference curves) depends on his economic experience. That is, a consumer who has temporarily experienced a different income or a different price constellation or a different consumption pattern (say, through advertising) will have a different set of consumption preferences when these temporary influences are removed than he had before. The consumer cannot decide what is his most preferred combination of commodities instantaneously, only after many trials and errors. But, by then, his income, the commodities available, the structure of prices, all will have changed and the process will go on continuously. What this means is that economic models, in addition to allowing for random errors arising from the process of measurement of consumer demand, should also incorporate random elements arising from the trial-and-error structure of consumer's choice. Going further, Georgescu-Roegen has pointed out that the groping manner in which a consumer decides what he prefers calls into question the basic mathematical assumption that the equations or curves representing consumer choice are analytical functions. That is, you cannot assume that because you can ascertain the relationship of quantity demanded to price for a small range of prices and quantities you can then compute the relationship over the whole range (Georgescu-Roegen, 1967, p. 181).

There are also kinds of behaviour change that result from interaction with others. A consumer may get pleasure by sacrificing his otherwise desired consumption pattern for others (i.e. behaviour inside a family, charitable contributions in response to a particular emergency). Then there is the *schadenfreude* that 'the Jones' get from awakening envy by adopting a conspicuous consumption pattern that others cannot keep up with. Taking this one ultimate step further, there is the perverse type of behaviour exemplified in Groucho Marx's famous remark, 'I wouldn't join any club that is willing to have someone like me as a member'.

The discussion so far has accepted the usual economic assumption that what is involved in consumer choice is the desire of a consumer to maximize satisfaction in selecting bundles of goods and services within the limitations set by the consumer's income. This is, as Scitovsky (1976) has shown, too simplistic an approach. Rather than the single motivation of the desire for satisfaction, there are three motive forces of behaviour: the drive to relieve discomfort, the desire for stimulation to relieve boredom, and the desire for the pleasure that can accompany and reinforce both. The single-variable satisfaction approach does not take into account the complexity, the varying mix of reinforcement and contradiction, that these three motives bring to bear on the calculus of individual choice. For example, one can get more of both comfort and stimulation up to a point, but beyond that point they come increasingly into conflict — more of one can be had only at the expense of the other: a luxurious car provides a great deal of comfort but it lulls the driver to sleep; a racing car keeps the senses to their highest pitch but comfort is hardly served. Comfort and pleasure also may reinforce or contradict each other. The satisfaction of a want eliminates a discomfort and gives pleasure but, as St Augustine commented 1,500 years ago, the initial presence of discomfort may be a necessary condition of pleasure. One must be cold to appreciate a good fire. Eating appeases hunger, but we must be hungry to get pleasure from eating. Unless we first deprive ourselves of food (not eat between meals, for example) we cannot get the maximum pleasure from food. A most important way to get pleasure from stimulation is through novelty. In other words, the desired consumption pattern of an individual is constantly changing because there is pleasure in the change and in variety *per se*. At times, pleasure can be derived from a change from change, particularly if it is felt to be too rapid. That is, there is pleasure in varying between much stimulation and little or no stimulation.

The basic postulate of consumer behaviour assumes that the consumer with a limited budget will cut his food consumption short of full satiation (in order to be able to purchase some other good). In fact, the *process* of satisfying a need is pleasurable in itself and strengthens carrying on the activity, often causing the consumer to continue to the point of full satisfaction and even beyond. Once the consumer starts eating, the sheer pleasure of the process may lead him to go on eating and order a dessert that earlier he judged he could neither afford nor want.

In the basic postulate no differentiation is made between preferences for goods that satisfy fundamental biological and physical needs (i.e. goods like the necessary minimum of food, clothing and shelter) and goods that meet cultural wants. That is, some goods are more directed to meeting the comfort drive and some the stimulation drive. The first set of goods meets preferences that are relatively much more constant and fixed and dominate consumption patterns in the less developed countries. But these latter wants (for cars, stereos, calculators, etc.) are practically open-ended and are constantly changing in response to the impact of advertising and events. The process of trial and error in a consumer's establishment of a complete preference ordering among all commodities open to him is therefore intensified and prolonged with economic development.

All of these different aspects of consumer behaviour affect different consumers differently. Individual variations are sufficiently great, once an economy gets beyond the satisfaction of basic needs, that it becomes difficult to identify a sufficient number of people with similar consumption patterns to construct accurate price indices. In the United States, it has proved impossible so far to identify any group of consumers that could be regarded as 'truly homogeneous' for price index purposes (Triplett, 1975, p. 66).

As a result of the increased proportion of discretionary purchases compared to purchases of vital necessities in higher income countries, George Katona (1975) has shown through extensive research that another element, 'consumer confidence', is important in affecting how the economy behaves. In the case of investment, it is fairly obvious that confidence, or what Keynes called 'animal spirits', of entrepreneurs affects its pace and size. But consumption was regarded by economists as being a function of personal disposable income. When predictions based on past calculated relationships of consumption to current personal disposable income proved wrong, refinements were proposed — among others that what mattered was people's estimates of their lifetime income. No evidence has been found that people do have expectations about their lifetime income or that consumers attempt to achieve a preferred distribution of consumption over their entire life. Empirical research has shown, however, that consumers' spending depends not only upon objective explanatory variables like disposable personal income but also on their 'willingness to spend'. This psychological factor is influenced by their confidence or the relative degree of optimism they feel about the future. The result is that predictions about the course of the economy based on surveys of consumer attitudes have often proved to be a more accurate guide than those cranked out of the macro-models with their fixed structural equations (Katona, 1975; Strumpel *et al.*, 1972).

One of the implicit assumptions of the basic postulate is that the consumer possesses all the necessary knowledge of what commodity bundles are available to him, what their qualities are and what their prices are. As we have seen in chapter 4, in the section on transaction costs, this knowledge cannot be taken as given. There are costs involved in securing this information and rational behaviour results in making in necessary decisions while knowledge is still rough and imperfect, since attaining perfect knowledge would cost more than the additional benefits expected.

There is another analytical approach here that also shows that consumers do not make a set of optimum choices among the commodities and services available to them. This is the result of what Herbert A. Simon (1979) has named 'bounded rationality'. Briefly, human beings are not omniscient; they do not know all the alternatives and must search for them. A consumer is not able to estimate exactly the marginal costs of and the returns from the search. Therefore, the consumer operates with some prior opinion about how good an alternative must be to satisfy his search. As soon as he discovers an alternative that meets his level of aspiration, he stops his search and settles on that alternative. In other words, a consumer 'satisfices' rather than optimizes.

'Bounded rationality', i.e. operating on the basis of a simplified model of the world because only so can one cope with it, is not limited to decisions influenced by incomplete knowledge. Kunreuther and Slovic have shown that it applies also to decisions about risk. People have a 'finite capacity of concern': there are only just so many dangers that they can worry about — the rest they put out of their mind. Consequently, while they insure against high-probability low-loss hazards, they do not take low-cost insurance against the rare catastrophe that would wipe them out (Kunreuther and Slovic, 1978, pp. 64 – 9).

Leibenstein has presented two additional arguments showing that the conventional approach is too deterministic. Almost as an aside, in his *Beyond Economic Man*, Leibenstein has demonstrated that the conventional postulate of diminishing marginal utility does not hold for certain classes of goods. These are 'target' goods, which may have zero utility up to a minimum target level and only be positive beyond that (for example, a medicine that is effective only in some minimum dosage). In the case of the degree of a medical doctor, the final instalment of completing the course is the difference between being able to engage in a lucrative profession or engaging in much inferior alternatives — marginal utility here being much greater than intra-marginal utility. Consequently, the curve of marginal utility of expenditure may be positively inclined at some part of the curve (Leibenstein, 1976, pp. 180 – 1).

Even if we had found that the economic behaviour of a single individual taken alone could be determined precisely, there is still the problem of how individuals behave when they are members of groups, formal or informal. The behaviour of a group or organization of human beings cannot be assumed to be simply the algebraic sum of the behaviour of the individual human beings when they are acting separately. As Knight points out, predicting the behaviour of groups has all the insuperable difficulties of predicting individual behaviour. Groups, like individuals, carry their past with them and grow in historical uniqueness. They are quite as sensitive and erratic as the individual (Knight, 1924, p. 254).

In more modern terms, the argument is that there are two main sets of individual behaviour characteristics: Type A, when the individual is acting essentially by himself, and Type B, when the individual is a member of a group or organization. The second set would cover (possibly in probability distributions) the choices and actions of each individual in the group or organization, in response to all the possible choices and actions of the other individuals or the consequences of them. The resultants of the second set of individual behaviour characteristics could then be considered to be logically equivalent to the behaviour characteristics of the group. Group behaviour, therefore, can be quite different from the summation of Type A individual behaviour characteristics. It also appears quite obvious that, except in very highly structured circumstances where Type B behaviour is strictly and absolutely limited to very few choices, attempting to predict group behaviour solely from studying individual behaviour patterns very quickly becomes unmanageable as the number of individuals in the group grows beyond a fairly small number (e.g. the number of possible outcomes with 10 individuals each having only two choices is 2^{10} or 1024). Yet this assumes that it *is* possible to ascertain exactly in advance what an individual's response is likely to be in response to all the possible variations in behaviour of other people and to all possible changes in the exogenous factors. However, the truth is more likely to be that, except in strictly limited circumstances, it is doubtful that any individual can predict beforehand exactly what even his own behaviour will be in response to a substantial change in the exogenous influences.

In a somewhat parallel argument, Hayek maintains that some economic phenomena are so *complex* that it is in practice impossible to get to know accurately all the factors that determine the outcome. In the physical sciences, it can be generally assumed that any important factor that determines the observed events will itself be observable and measurable. This is not so in some parts of economic life. In a market, for example, the determination of prices and wages is affected by the particular information possessed by every one of the participants in the market — a sum of facts that in their totality cannot be known to the observer (Hayek, 1975, p. 35).

The cumulative effect of all this discussion is that the basic postulate of consumer behaviour cannot be regarded as anything more than a rough approximation to a complicated economic reality. It is in essence a loose concept: it gives a rough — that is, not precise — grasp of the elusive changing truth. We can use it in analysis of a problem, but the analysis cannot be highly sophisticated; it has to be simple and rough.

Theory of the firm

Over the last century the structure of the economy in the presently industrialized countries has profoundly altered. Compared to the earlier period (and to the less developed countries today), when the economy was made up of a multitude of small farmers, shop-keepers and small businesses, the industrialized economies today are highly organized into the dominant business form of the corporation (Mason, 1959, 'Introduction'; Marris and Mueller, 1980). In the United States, for example, 1300 corporations pro-duce three-quarters of total corporate net income after taxes. In manufacturing, the 200 largest corporations controlled 60 per cent of all assets in 1977, up from 45 per cent in 1945 (Herman, 1981, p. 1). In the state centralized planning economies of the Soviet Union and Eastern Europe, the various state trusts are even more dominant. In the modern industrialized countries, consequently, most adults now are wage and salaried employees working for large organizations. In the large corporations, the nominal owners, the shareholders, are generally passive with real control typically in the hands of professional management, which selects its own replacements.

The discussion so far has essentially accepted what scientists call reductionism. This is the belief that a whole can be understood completely if you understand its parts and the nature of their sum. (The opposite point of view, 'holism', maintains instead that things can be understood only as wholes, not as sums of their parts.) Reductionism in economics argues, as we have seen, that the basic postulate on which one must build is the behaviour of the individual. But, as Frank Knight argues, reductionism rigorously applied cannot stop there; he suggests that analysis has to go down to the invariant and measurable human traits such as reflexes (Knight, 1956, p. 176). By analogy with the hard sciences, one could go further and say that to determine exactly the conduct of an individual we must understand what controls the action of the neurons of his brain that determine his behaviour. We must have an equation describing the behaviour of each of the 10 billion neurons that eventually result in a particular economic decision. But once we have these equations we are still not finished. The behaviour of each cell cannot be completely understood until we have an equation describing the behaviour of the macro-molecules of which it is composed. And so we could continue on downwards, level by level, until ultimately we arrive at what now appears to be the lowest level — the quarks, which, if they really exist, make up the protons and neutrons in the atom's nucleus.

To be a thoroughgoing rigorous reductionist and to maintain that a scientific deterministic economic theory must ultimately be built up from the sets of equations that describe the behaviour of quarks is obviously absurd. The way out is to use the analytical approach of hierarchical levels used by natural scientists. As we move up to each new level, we need additional principles, which neither deny nor contradict the explanations appropriate for lower levels. The idea of having partially independent hierarchical levels of explanation is basically intuitive common sense.

The approach, then, is that at each higher level we summarize (or 'chunk') in manageable capsule form a number of things that at the lower, more detailed level are seen as separate. And for these capsules or chunks we need new additional principles to explain their behaviour. (The basic 'chunk' concept comes from Miller's truly seminal paper, 'The Magical Number Seven, Plus or Minus Two' (1956).) For example, to understand words we need to know more than the letters of the alphabet; to work with water we need to know more than that hydrogen and oxygen are toxic gases. An effective atomic theory works with a chunked concept of an atomic nucleus that is derived from but is something more than a nuclear physicist's theory. In this way, in economics we can work with a theory of the behaviour of individuals without having to know the specific details of molecular or atomic particle behaviour several levels below. (Our knowledge of individual behaviour is nevertheless enriched by the research on the details of how the human brain's neurons actually work. A considerable industry now exists for producing chemicals — e.g. tranquillizers, lithium, phenothiazines — that an individual may resort to in order to modify his behaviour as a person through influencing his brain's neurons; see the report on artificial intelligence in Hofstadter, 1979.)

Further, by analogy, we can legitimately move to a level higher and develop chunked theories of the economic behaviour of economic organizations such as corporations and trade unions. Such a theory can provide insights and descriptions of corporate behaviour, for example, that could never be attained through attempting the aggregation of the individual behaviour equations concerned. Biologists have found that an ant colony or a bee hive behaves with a higher level of intelligence than the summation of the intelligence of the individual ants or bees. In chemistry, Boyle's

Law relates pressures, volume and temperature of a gas without the necessity for the chemist to compute the behaviour of each individual molecule. In fact, the relationship among these three concepts is meaningless at the level of a molecule and could never be developed by simply studying the behaviour of an individual molecule alone. Similarly, an integrated irrigation system has to be analysed as a unit; analysis at the level of an individual farmer alone is meaningless. At the level of the corporation, new economic principles like those developed by Leibenstein (see below) become necessary to grasp economic behaviour.

But chunking does not come without cost. While it makes analysis and data manageable, the reductionists are right that this is attained with a loss in determinism. In the case of some physical systems, the sub-systems that are chunked to make up a system are sufficiently reliable and can be sufficiently predicted from their chunked description that the system itself is virtually deterministic. (A brick wall made up of bricks and mortar is a good example.) But this is not true of human individuals or of sub-groups and groups of human individuals. Consequently, as we move to higher levels of chunking or of organizations of human beings (from the one-man firm, to the industrial plant, to the division, to the corporation, to the sector, to the economy), the system loses at each level some element of determinism and predictability. If our economic model of reality is to be isomorphic with reality, it must therefore also lose in determinism and predictability — it increasingly becomes able only to predict probabilities of ending up in certain abstract spaces of behaviour and is far from the precision of prediction of physics. (We shall see this principle exemplified in this section.)

The modern corporation has replaced the market as the way in which labour and capital are directly allocated to future productive processes and the flow of goods is coordinated through existing processes of production and distribution (see Chandler's basic work on this, 1977). The managers of a corporation are the most important decision-makers in the economy. They are salaried, are not the legal owners and typically hold at most a minute percentage of the shares of the corporation they serve. The managers usually control the appointments of the directors or themselves serve as members of the boards of directors to whom they are supposed to be responsible. The managers of a corporation have their own set of motivations that may not coincide with those of the owners and may, in fact, conflict with them. Lawyers know, for instance, that if they have a corporation-caused injury it is preferable *not* to identify the particular manager responsible and try to collect from him. If they sue an officer in his own name he will fight like a tiger; the money he is being asked to pay comes from his own pocket. But when he is settling on behalf of the corporation, he will be more forthcoming; the money he is paying out is the corporations's, not his own (C. Stone, 1976, p. 59).

How well corporate managers do their job is critical to the performance of a modern industrialized economy. Very little work has been done by economists on this nor does conventional economic theory have much to say on the theory of the corporation. In conventional theory, a firm gets the necessary information from the market in the prices of its inputs (labour, capital, raw materials, etc.) and of its output. The relationship between the amounts of inputs needed for particular outputs is set by a fixed production function. The firm decides on its output and the needed inputs by following a single decision rule — maximizing its profit. The whole process is neat, precise and deterministic (Cyert and Hedrick, 1972, p. 398).

Many economists have no difficulty in recognizing that a goverment bureaucracy can act as an interest group (or congeries of groups) pushing its own special ends that may run counter to those of the efficient functioning of the economy or of the general good of society. But most economists refuse to extend this insight to corporate managements because the profit-maximization objective within a competitive market is supposed to keep managers working for the benefit of society as a whole.

In spite of the discouraging attitude of most economists, there have been a significant number of attempts in recent years to bring more realism into the theory of the firm. I am not going to attempt to survey the work here or to make any contribution to it; I am merely going to try to indicate how this work fits into the general theme of this book.

M. A. Adelman, an economist who believes that the major objective of corporation managements is to maximize the profits of the corporation, but who is also highly knowledgeable about economic reality, does not accept the assumption that efficient decision-making by the management will naturally place the firm on the production frontier boundary where profits are maximum. Adelman graphically describes the corporate management in the effort towards maximizing profit as '. . . struggling through a viscous fluid of inertia and misunderstanding toward that boundary, which does not even have the grace to stay put. Information about the boundary comes often as a kick in the slats: sales are being lost, profits dwindling. . .' (Adelman, 1972, p. 494).

The top management of a corporation, even if it is a profit-maximizer (and we shall see that there is considerable evidence that not all are), has the discretion to decide how the 'profits' shall be divided between the shareholders and the management. In the latter case, as we saw in chapter 5, 'profits' diverted to pay for various 'perks' of management become converted into costs. In many cases there is a considerable leeway in the division of the benefits from operations. It is not easy to come by information on what is actually decided since management has an interest to conceal it. Managers of management-controlled firms often attempt to control the data presented in annual accounting reports in a manner that causes firm performance to be misrepresented (Salamon and Smith, 1979). (If a shareholder comes to feel that shareholders are being unfairly treated by the corporation, his option to sell his shares may simply be an option to take a second loss in the price of the shares.) In the United States, the Securities and Exchange Commission (SEC) from to time exposes some extreme examples of management abuse of this discretion.

There have been a number of economists who have found that maximizing profits is not an accurate description of the major objective of corporations (see survey by Marris and Mueller, 1980). These economists have advanced the idea of a more complex set of objectives: Scitovsky suggests that entrepreneurs would trade income for leisure as their incomes rise; Baumol emphasizes sales-maximization as an objective, but subject to earning some desired level of profits; Marris finds growth-maximization to be the objective of the corporations he studied, but with sufficient profits to prevent threats of displacement to the managers; Williamson takes profit-maximization as the objective but only after the managers have taken care of their desire for various 'perks', including taking it easier than otherwise. These theories suggest that, instead of maximizing a unique profits objective function, managers maximize a utility function with more than one argument, with the different arguments varying from corporation to corporation and subject to the constraint imposed by the opportunity set they face. This amounts to little more than using technical jargon to say that managers do what they do.

These theories are an attempt to make the conventional theory more realistic and are based on findings from empirical work. There is considerable evidence that they are all true — applying in different degrees to different corporations and probably varying over time — but that they account for only part of the different objectives pursued by different corporations. An investigation by Robert F. Lanzillotti (1958) over several years into the specific objectives that corporations actually had in making their price decisions found different corporations had different objectives. American Can, Kroger, Standard Oil of Indiana and Swift all wanted merely to maintain their share of the market. Goodyear, Gulf and National Steel regarded themselves as price followers — they matched their major competitors' price changes. A. & P. and Sears, Roebuck tried to increase their market share. Alcoa, du Pont, Esso, General Electric, General Motors and International Harvester tried to secure a target rate of return on their investment (but this varied from firm to firm, from 10 per cent to 20 per cent after taxes). General Foods' objective was to have a 33⅓ per cent gross margin on sales. Stabilization of prices was the major objective of Kennecott and a secondary objective of several other corporations (Alcoa, American Can, Esso). Only Johns Manville had something like the conventional profit-maximization objective: it wanted to increase its return on investment over its last 15-year average (about 15 per cent after taxes), but it wanted to do this *without increasing* its market share above 20 per cent.

In the American automobile industry until the early 1980s, when foreign imports began to stimulate price competition, the general policy was to set prices based on a fixed sales forecast. The company pricing committee would forecast how many cars they expected to sell without reference to a price. They then estimated total costs, added the desired profit margins and calculated the average sales price by dividing the total cost-plus-profits by projected unit sales. If total costs rose or sales fell, car prices would be raised (Koten and Bennett, 1981, p. 1).

In the real economy, it seems clear that corporation actions are not determined by any single decision rule of profit-maximization.

Corporate managements have a set of competing objectives, the choice or combination of choices varying from corporation to corporation: one management will choose the 'easy life', another will seek to grow by aggressively increasing its market share or by developing new markets, etc. During the inflation of the late 1970s and early 1980s, corporate managements found it attractive to expand by using corporate cash and credit to buy control of other corporations. With low share prices, it was often cheaper to acquire assets in this way than by investment in new plant and equipment. But in some cases, it was also quite clear that the acquisitions were motivated more by personal egos of chief corporate officers wanting to build an empire than by the interests of the shareholders of the corporations they were in charge of. In one notorious American case, each of two corporations tried to swallow the other and finally the one that started the fight was swallowed by a third that was brought in as a 'white knight' to ensure a friendly takeover. The financial ratings of all three corporations suffered as a result.

Corporate policy objectives will change with change in management personnel over time and with changes in the external environment. Lanzillotti's conclusions from his valuable but neglected contribution are that no single theory of the firm and no single hypothesis such as profit-maximization is likely to result in unambiguous course of action for the firm in any given situation or to provide a satisfactory basis for valid predictions of price behaviour (Lanzillotti, 1958, pp. 938 – 9).

We have already touched on H. A. Simon's concepts of 'satisficing' and 'bounded rationality' in the discussion on the theory of the consumer. These are not just 'loose concepts'; their strength lies in their recognition of the realism of the looseness attribute of the concept. They apply equally well to the decision-making of a firm. In the conventional theory, once the environment is given, the assumption of perfect rationality and profit-maximization fully determines how the firm will behave. In Simon's behavioural theory of rational choice (1979), the outcome of a firm's behaviour cannot be precisely predicted. A firm, under this approach, makes decisions that it regards as good enough — given its limited knowledge, its limited predictive power and its limited computational power.

So far the discussion has departed from the usual unstated

economics assumption that the firm can be treated as though it were a homogeneous economic unit analogous to an individual producer only by recognizing that the management may have interests distinct from that of the corporation proper. But this is not the end of the story. Central to how close and how efficiently a corporation comes to the objectives of its top management is the effectiveness with which the top management is able to get its decisions implemented by the middle managers — who may number in the tens of thousands — and the rest of the staff — who may number in the hundreds of thousands and who may be distributed in plants and offices around the globe. This is what schools of business management are largely about. The great development of organizational forms and management techniques over the last 140 years has made possible the modern corporation with its multitude of individual administrative and production units supervised by a hierarchy of thousands of middle and top managers. Even with all the modern techniques and management aids, it is still true that the results cannot be uniquely determined by top management decisions.

In a series of articles and a book (1976, 1977, 1978a, b, 1979), Harvey Leibenstein has developed the seminal 'X-inefficiency' theory, which provides a much more realistic and coherent explanation of economic behaviour *within* corporations than the old simplistic maximizing assumption. Economists have been trained to assume that people always optimize. A firm, for example, since it wants to maximize profits, will secure the maximum possible output at the lowest possible costs from the given quantities of productive factors. Leibenstein (1976) shows that there are good reasons to believe that this is not an appropriate assumption in analysing the behaviour of firms and calls the indeterminate shortfall between the theoretical optimum and what actually results 'X-inefficiency'. In other words, optimization within a firm is, in my terms, a loose concept. That is, the conventional model assumes behaviour is precisely determined at the optimum while in reality it is somewhere short of that in the imprecise grey area.

Most economic production in industrialized countries is carried out in organized groups — corporations in mixed economies, trusts in communist countries. Conventional theory assumes a worker is paid according to his contribution to the product. But in large organizations, wages are based on workers' classification in job categories and their seniority, and fringe benefits may largely depend merely on membership in the system. All that a worker has to do is maintain some tolerable minimum of performance to stay within the system (Katz, 1972, p. 59). Leibenstein points out that all workers have varying degrees of discretion in the amount and quality of effort they put into carrying out their jobs. There is no reason why each worker should try always to work in such a way as to maximize the output of the group. Anyone who has ever had managerial responsibilities will recognize the truth of this approach: a major responsibility of a manager is to persuade, coerce or in some way motivate each individual to make an effort to approach his or her optimum output. There is a whole apparatus of regular systematic personnel evaluations in most large organizations directed towards trying to ascertain how each individual should be judged on this basis. What is clear is that, except for workers on assembly-line operations, it is usually extremely difficult to judge whether a worker, supervisor, middle or top manager is producing optimally in relation to the objectives set by top management. Anyone who has ever worked in a large organization knows that frequently people are paid identical salaries but are producing very different amounts of work (Clague, 1977, p. 83).

In spite of all their coercive apparatus, the Soviet managers have similar problems. In November 1978, President Brezhnev complained, 'What good was the plan if projects never get finished; if, for instance, a tin-can factory in Nakhodka begun in 1966 would not be completed until 1983?'

The large corporations handle the problem of managing large masses of employees and capital by dividing them into units and sub-units. This is unavoidable and is an effective technique of management but it has also carried with it the drawback that the units then develop their own sets of objectives, loyalties and morale. These provide another element of slack in carrying out the objectives of top management and, at times, can directly conflict with the objectives set for the overall organization. To a lesser or greater extent, a corporation is actually a battleground in which the different functional units (production, sales, finance, research) are in constant conflict with each other for their own particular objectives. The management hierarchy is involved in trying to contain, resolve and compromise the conflicts. In the end, no one individual or department optimizes in the usual sense (Kornai, 1971, ch. 7). In the early years of the World Bank, various organizational schemes were tried. Finally, in 1952, the top management team of Eugene Black and Robert Garner deliberately structured the organization so that there would be a continuing conflict between the projects staff and the area desks. In this way, the projects engineers and analysts would battle to get good projects and good project policies out of governments while the area departments fought to get loans made. In George Woods' presidency, he set up a new economics department deliberately to create a new conflict area in order to try to secure more emphasis in Bank operations on economic development policy. In the internal organization of General Motors, the president of the corporation is supposed to be a production man and to represent the interests of the production divisions, while the chairman represents the financial side of the business. There is consequently built-in an actual or latent conflict within top management itself.

Thus the microeconomics and the possibility of free play within the different parts of the corporation do not necessarily lead to precise maximizing. Maximizing behaviour is an extreme and in reality a practically non-existent case. Individuals and organizational units in a firm do not necessarily or usually pursue gains to a maximum degree or marshal information optimally. Since a firm cannot completely control the amount of effort individuals and its organizational units expend, it cannot necessarily minimize costs. The firm can be regarded as an arena in which there is a struggle between cost-raising tendencies as individuals and sub-units pursue their own ends and the cost-containing activities of top management.

Even a competitive environment may not result in firms operating at lowest costs because there may be a lack of the right kind of new entrepreneur. For example, if the existing X-inefficiency is 20 per cent above minimum cost, there may be no entrepreneurs who believe they could enter and produce at a lower cost. Also, the existing firms may substitute market-sheltering (price competition reducing) activities for attempts to reduce X-inefficiency — i.e. advertise to establish consumer acceptance of a brand name rather than try to cut costs. Monopolistic firms are likely to have higher costs than the average competitive firms because the pressure on management to struggle to contain costs is less.

Corporations, in short, do not operate on the optimum production frontier. Output and costs in a firm are not deterministic and cannot be represented by results with definite fixed single points but can vary widely depending upon a number of motivational factors specific to individuals and to organizational units and the relationships among these in the specific firm.

The discussion so far applies as much to socialist economies as it does to the mixed economies. The centrally planned economies have additional X-inefficiency elements. The planners are even further removed from the individual workers than corporate top managements. In relation to the enterprise managers, the planners do not have sufficient detailed knowledge of the enterprise's production functions and are dependent to a large degree on the information provided by each enterprise of its capabilities. This clearly sets up a two-person game situation. This is intensified because planning in the Soviet Union is based on the 'ratchet principle' — the plan for next year is based on this year's output plus an increment. Since both the manager and workers in a particular plant are aware that over-fulfilment of their plan will result in their being given higher plan targets in future years, they have a strong incentive to expend less than their maximum effort.

Kantorovich, the noted Soviet mathematical economist, got the Egorov railway-carriage plant in trouble: by persuading the management to use his linear programming methods, the plant achieved an unexpected output of 94 per cent of capacity. The next year the plant was ordered to increase its output by 7 per cent to 101 per cent of capacity and Kantorovich and the plant manager narrowly escaped being considered saboteurs when they tried to persuade the planners that this was impossible! (Katsenelinboigen, 1978 – 79, p. 134).

A Soviet writer comments that 'the striving of the lower levels to hide their productive possibilities' conceals big reserves for the potential growth of the economy if this effort-gap could be eliminated (Loeb and Magat, 1978, p. 173).

In sum, whether in a Western corporation or in an East European government trust, for a particular set of inputs (labour, capital, level of technology, raw materials, energy) the volume and costs of output are not uniquely determined but rather can be expected to vary considerably from enterprise to enterprise and over time.

9

Welfare Economics and Cost – Benefit Analysis

> Economic welfare is a subject in which rigor and refinement are probably worse than useless. Rough theory, or good common sense, is, in practice, what we require.
>
> I. M. D. Little, *A Critique of Welfare Economics*

Welfare economics is the branch of economics that attempts to provide an analysis by which society can decide which economic alternatives open to it are better or worse on an economically rational basis. (Whole books have been written to try to work out more fully what this definition means. I found Little (1957) and Mishan (1967, 1971) most useful. In discussing a most difficult subject, both are remarkably clear writers.) If perfect competition existed for all economic activities and all effects that are relevant to the welfare of individuals were priced through this perfect market, then it can be shown that individuals' pursuit of their own selfish economic interests would also bring about maximum social benefit. The same optimum results could also be achieved if the economy were completely directed by an all-wise central economic planner who was motivated to make all the correct economic decisions for the economy. It is self-evident that these optimum conditions describe a kind of economist's Utopia or science fiction construct — they never have existed nor ever will exist. (The text represents what I believe can be derived as useful policy guidance from welfare economics. Formal welfare economic theory has in recent years become so refined that there is practically no substance of use left to it. The general consensus has been to focus on the 'social welfare function'. That is, social welfare is a function of the personal utility levels. Kenneth Arrow (1974a) has shown that, on the basis of the usual conditions laid down for this function, it is *impossible* that a function exists that satisfies these conditions (see, Sen (1979).)

In a large part of the existing mixed economies, decisions on how economic resources are allocated are guided more or less by the private profit motive within a market environment that differs to a greater or less degree from perfect competition. In the 'grants economy' part, resources are allocated according to various charitable, religious and benevolent motives. Finally, there is the part of the economy where resources are allocated by administrations that need to be guided by some consideration of social benefits and costs. (The same divisions exist in today's centrally planned economies, but the proportions are likely to be quite different from those of a mixed economy.)

One of the lessons derived from welfare economics is that there are spillover effects (external benefits or costs) from economic decisions that are not included in the internal accounting of the particular enterprise or project making the decisions (e.g. pollution of a river by a paper plant). So that even in a market private enterprise part of an economy, it may be necessary for a government to take action to be sure that social costs and benefits are taken into consideration in the making of allocation decisions.

Both welfare economics and cost – benefit analysis, which is based on it, are inherently imprecise. Once the perfect competition Utopia is left behind and the problems of the real world are considered, welfare economics essentially comes down to the following proposition: an economic change is desirable if it (a) would result in a good redistribution of wealth, i.e. reduce the extremes of wealth and poverty, and (b) would make one or more people better off without making anyone worse off. (The latter condition is often restated as: 'any potential losers could not profitably bribe the potential gainers to oppose the change'; in other words, the loss to the potential losers is less than the gain to the potential gainers.)

Condition (a) would be repudiated by many, perhaps most, economists. As we have seen in the preceding chapter, the basic postulate of consumer behaviour assumes that a consumer can and does make *intra-personal* comparisons of the utilities of the goods and services available to him. However, conventional economics also assumes that one cannot make *inter-personal* comparisons of utilities. Since one cannot add utilities, one cannot say whether Jones or Smith is better off no matter what their respective incomes are. In other words, while the theory of value is based on the assumption that other people's psychology is much like that of oneself, this assumption is abandoned when it comes to comparing the welfare of different people (Blaug, 1980, p. 89). The discussion in the preceding chapter showed that the fundamental postulate is only roughly true, does not provide precise results and therefore, justifies the belief that one cannot measure differences in utilities or welfare between individuals — where those differences are small. But from our loose concepts logic we can see that, as one goes towards the extremes, it is absurd to maintain that it is impossible to ascertain whether a billionaire is better off than a starving African peasant.

There are several other logical problems in cost – benefit analysis that make it inherently imprecise, in addition to the empirical difficulties that will be discussed later in this chapter. In every case, Little points out, the exact application of the theory assumes eternal and perfectly consistent individuals, who choose between infinitely divisible goods of unchanging quality. This unreality does not '. . . make the conclusions of the theory worthless, but does make it silly to treat them as anything but rough guides to practice' (Little, 1957, p. 278).

Then there is the problem of the theory of the 'second-best'. (As indicated above, it is absurd to assume that there is or ever will be any economy characterized by the optimum conditions that would make possible first-best economic decisions.) Economic theorists have shown that if there is some departure from optimum conditions, then the necessary conditions to obtain maximum social welfare are much more complicated. That is to say, if there is general misallocation of resources in an economy, even if one could know what the optimal prices should be in the whole economy, putting these first-best prices in effect in just one sector would not act towards maximizing social welfare. If prices in an economy are 40 per cent above marginal cost, then social welfare is increased not by the first-best solution of setting prices in one sector at marginal cost but by the second-best solution of setting prices here too at 40 per cent above marginal cost.

It is not likely that a cost – benefit analyst will be able to calculate an exact second-best solution for any industry or project that he is working on. However, he can still get some guidance from the general propositions of welfare economics. That is, by trying to get a so-called 'Pareto improvement', he can try to make decisions that will result in as much additional output as possible without increasing any input or reducing other outputs. (There is a logical difficulty in cost – benefit analysis, first discovered by Scitovsky, that has never been resolved. It is another example of the difficulty that economics has in trying to capture reality within the framework of economic concepts. It is logically possible, say, to have a project A that has a greater net social benefit than Project B, Project B that has a greater net social benefit than Project C, while Project C has a greater net social benefit than Project A. This basically comes about because as the economy changes from a situation with Project A to the situation with Project B etc., the tastes of different consumers acquire different weights in determining prices, which then change too (de V. Graaff, 1975, pp. 237 – 40; Mishan, 1971, pp. 319 – 21).

Fairly early in the evolution of development economics after World War II, it became widely accepted among economists that markets in the less developed countries were so imperfect that market prices (including wage rates, foreign exchange rates and interest rates) were not reliable guides to an optimal allocation of economic resources. Consequently, if better decisions were to be made, economists would have to calculate the special economic parameters that would have to be used. A second complication has been added in recent years in that leading economists in the field, sponsored by international organizations, have broadly agreed that special adjustments had also to be made in the course of the calculations to secure social objectives such as improving income distribution and accelerating growth through encouraging saving. Under the new World Bank methodology (Squire and van der Tak, 1975), the first set of adjustments of market prices is called 'efficiency analysis', and the second, 'social analysis'. In 'efficiency analysis', essentially what is done is the computation of a set of 'shadow' prices ('accounting' prices) to be used in place of market prices in the cost – benefit analysis of a project. In the 'social analysis' step, the Little and Mirrlees (1968), UNIDO (1972), and new World Bank methodology (Squire and van der Tak, 1975) all attempt to bring social objectives into the cost – benefit analysis by attaching appropriate weights to the different private costs and benefits.

Applying cost – benefit analysis in practice is inescapably imprecise; practically all the factors that cause imprecision in economic data and applied economic analysis are involved in cost – benefit analysis:

(1) The results depend on estimates of future outputs, future costs, future prices and how long the future stream of outputs may last. The fuzziness in estimates of expected output and costs resulting from the operation of Leibenstein's X-inefficiency is, of course, involved; this is why appraisal of the management of the project is so important.

(2) If output of the project is not marketed, the valuation to be placed on it is a matter of judgement and realistically cannot be precise.

(3) If output is sold, only very rarely can one be sure of the future price it will bring. If output is priced by the market, do private and social benefits coincide? If not, the latter cannot be measured precisely.

(4) The problems of estimating what is the proper opportunity cost of capital to use are well known, and equally well known is the conclusion that no completely acceptable, much less precise, way of estimating this key parameter has yet been found (Schmedtje, 1965). (The alternative, even more complex, way of discounting future benefits and costs, recommended by the UNIDO *Guidelines* (1972), at the end runs into the same difficulty of calculating precisely the marginal productivity of capital as does the opportunity cost of capital approach.)

(5) The currently recommended methodology of cost – benefit analysis of projects is based on converting all costs and benefits into *border* prices rather than using domestic prices (see Little and Mirrlees, 1968, 1974; UNIDO, 1972; Squire and van der Tak, 1975). The preceding chapter on balance of payments gave a brief analysis of the many sources of inaccuracy that affect trade statistics and, therefore, any estimate of border prices drawn from them.

Guisinger and Papageorgiou point out that in fact no product has a unique price that is constant over time and that is universally known to all potential buyers and sellers. As a result, the belief that a single border price can be associated with each tradable good is a fiction (1976, p. 80). Kravis and Lipsey in their studies of export prices have shown that substantial differences exist in export prices (as high as 43 per cent in the case of iron and steel wire, for example) and persist over long periods (1977, p. 156). Guisinger and Papageorgiou go on to say that one can easily conceive of developing some composite price based on the average of the prices for the same commodity in different markets and at different times. In practice, it is difficult to know which transactions are relevant and which not — prices will vary according to different perceptions of risk and uncertainty by buyers and sellers, different sizes of transactions, etc.

Another element of imprecision is that an actual price quoted is often really the price of a bundle that consists of the basic product and all the associated product-related services such as suppliers' credit, packaging, promotional assistance by the seller, technical advice and warranties. It is practically impossible therefore to estimate what the border price for a product alone should be, eliminating these services. It is also not possible to make proper exact adjustments for differences in quality when the exact value of the quality difference is complicated by the price adjustments for the product-related services.

Guisinger and Papageorgiou attempted to gather information on the border prices of a few textile products in Nigeria from the various available sources. What they found was a fairly broad spread of prices for the same commodity for the same period. Even eliminating the extreme estimates, the range was around 100 – 200. Furthermore, it was impossible to ascertain precisely why the different sources disagreed. (These findings are quite obvious to anyone who has had substantial hands-on experience in business operations. But because economists tend to think of prices as scalars rather than as vectors, the results do appear unexpected.)

(6) No acceptable way of measuring returns in the social sectors has yet been found. In drinking water projects, Jeremy Warford (the World Bank's economic adviser in the sector) has pointed out, everyone acknowledges the health benefits of piped water supply, but '. . . not only are we unaware of the effects of improved water supply on health in monetary terms, we do not even know what the *physical* benefits are' (1971, p. 1). In education and training, the position is similar. As John Dunlop puts it, enormous research has been done on measuring the rates of return on training and edu-

cation. Virtually all this is irrelevant to policy-making and to the allocations of funds for training and education. 'Further, in my experience, decisions in these fields have been made in fact without regard to such formalistic and quantitative analysis . . .' (Dunlop, 1977, p. 9). The World Bank, after trying very hard to find some quantifiable way of assessing economic benefits from education and training projects, gave up the attempt, and its project decisions in this sector have been made on general policy considerations and cost-effectiveness analysis.

(7) Technical cooperation programmes are a substantial portion of the international aid and development bank programmes. No real attempt is made to apply cost – benefit analysis to these.

(8) No one has yet been able to devise a system that can identify and quantify precisely the exact weights to apply in the 'social analysis phase of cost – benefit analysis'. One cannot rely on policy statements of the government to provide precise guidance on this: policy statements are vague and often in conflict with the actual policies, and different parts of government may have different views and different policies. When policies are specific they cannot logically provide the basis because social cost – benefit analysis is in part justified by the constraints on government policies. How does one decide which policies represent constrained behaviour, and which unconstrained? The choice is essentially arbitrary (Stewart, 1978, p. 255). Even if a government did lay down a precise system of weights to use, there is still the judgement to make whether this particular government can and does identify exactly the social welfare function of its citizens. Even if one assumes a democratic government could do so (and democratic governments are often elected on other bases than their ability to determine exactly the community social welfare function), how many democratic governments are there in the less developed countries?

(I. M. D. Little, in his thoughtful *Critique of Welfare Economics*, argues that it is highly undemocratic to take the position that even a democratic government always knows what is best for its citizens and that it alone can say what is in the public interest (1957, pp. 120 – 1). In his later works on cost – benefit analysis, Little's position is exactly the opposite: he seems to have no doubts that any government can establish social weights for investment decisions. (Little and Mirrlees, 1968, 1974). In the final analysis, if some set of social weights is used, the most one can say is that they represent someone's best guess — more or less disguised as a scientific finding — based on his own set of social values, of what the national social priorities should be.)

(9) An investment programme of a government will usually include projects in industry or agriculture with a marketed output, economic infrastructure projects with some projects like roads with no marketed output, and social projects like schools. The degree of precision in applying cost – benefit analysis is highest in the first category but completely vanishes by the time it is attempted in the last category. Cost – benefit analysis can provide only limited guidance, therefore, to the allocation of investment resources among some sectors, not at all among others and none at all overall.

The conclusion has to be that cost – benefit analysis should be recognized as inherently imprecise. This does not, however, deny the value of this type of analysis — even rough estimates are better than arbitrary, politically determined or purely intuitive decisions. The value of cost – benefit analysis is that it forces an analyst to look at a project in the wider economic and social context, to try to identify and to estimate all the significant costs and benefits — both directly pertaining to the project and spilling over into the rest of the economy. The result of this disciplined process must be better knowledge of the project and its alternatives and, consequently, better investment decisions on balance over the longer run. But there is a serious question whether attempts to go beyond rough estimates, which will perform the function of weeding out the bad projects, are worthwhile and not misleading.

10

'Capital' and 'Investment' in Less Developed Countries

> Although capital would seem to have an easily accessible intuitive meaning, it is the most elusive concept in economics.
>
> Oskar Morgenstern, *On the Accuracy of Economic Observations*
>
> . . . it is advisable to place reliance upon rough estimates of the relevant concepts than on more exact estimates of irrelevant ones.
>
> E. J. Mishan, *Cost – Benefit Analysis*

In chapter 5 on national income and product accounts, we mentioned in passing that the definitions of 'capital' and 'investment' are among the debatable conventions used in national accounting. In this chapter we shall explore what the problems are with the conventional definitions and what might more usefully be put in their place. (The concept of capital and its relation to economic development and growth has been fought over by generations of economists and there is a vast literature on it that does not need to be cited here. Both T. Morgan (1969) and Wilson (1979) have useful sets of references.) The focus will be mostly on the less developed countries because there the drawbacks to the current conventions can be seen more clearly and are a greater handicap to making good economic policy decisions.

In the standard system of national accounts, investment consists of business enterprises' expenditures on physical capital goods (that is, durable assets such as buildings or machinery that have a life of over one year plus the annual change in business inventories or stocks of goods) and household purchases of houses. Professor Zvi Griliches, after carefully exploring the problems of the measurement of capital stock in investment functions, concludes that two different measures are needed: one 'approximating the idea of capital as a quantity of machines' and the other 'approximating the idea of capital as the current value of the existing stock of machines'. Griliches goes on to say that these two measures will offset gross investment in opposite directions (Griliches, 1963, pp. 135 – 6). While this argument robs the measurement of 'capital' of any pretence to a high degree of precision, in this chapter I shall try to show that neither of these two measures is fully adequate and that the problem of precise measurement is still more difficult.

The dominant and orthodox economic theory emphasizes capital formation as the main factor in development of the developing countries. This theory is taught to most students and has been the basis of most comprehensive economic development plans prepared by developing countries. Tinbergen, for example, recommends that the first step in development planning should be a macroeconomic study of the general process of production and investment along the lines suggested by Harrod – Domar models or by similar, more complicated models (Tinbergen and Bos, 1962, p. 10). In the Harrod – Domar model, growth in production is the result of a propensity to save and a fairly stable aggregate capital – output ratio. Consequently, the development of long-run planning models has focused on what have been regarded as the main limitations to growth: capital stock and foreign exchange to supplement savings in increasing capital stock (Chenery *et al.*, 1974, p. 183).

Helping countries to grow through the provision of foreign exchange to finance investment in material capital is the theoretical basis of the operations of the international development financing agencies, such as the World Bank Group, the Inter-American Development Bank, the Asian Development Bank, and so on. When these banks point with pride to their accomplishments, the volume of money that they have provided to finance an increase in the stock of material capital in the developing countries is in the centre of the stage for all to applaud. This preoccupation with physical capital goods is embedded in the World Bank's practice, policy and 'theology'. For example, the Bank's Articles of Agreement make financing the import component of the investment in a project the normal method of finance for the Bank. What the

Bank's board of directors recognizes as the 'proper' object of finance for the Bank is material capital goods imported from abroad needed for a 'high-priority' project. A substantial part of the economic battles in the Bank turn around this point. If, for one reason or another, the import of real resources to supplement local savings in a country is not sufficiently embodied in machinery or equipment, or if the durable capital goods the country does import are not used by the project that deserves financing, the Bank staff have to show that there are 'exceptional circumstances' to justify either the finance of local currency expenditure or a 'programme' loan, or adopt some roundabout method to achieve the Bank's objective.

There are good reasons why the definition of investment as expenditure on material capital goods has been adopted and used by economists. It descends from English classical economics and was strengthened by Keynes' *General Theory*. As Joan Robinson points out, Keynes' analysis was framed in terms of a short period in which the stock of capital and the techniques of production are given (1965, p. 2). Within this given structure of the economy, the definition of investment as expenditure on fixed capital was quite sufficient. It is not only a simple definition, easy for anyone to understand, but until recently, for the major purposes of economic policy in the developed countries, it was a perfectly adequate and useful definition. It also has a popular appeal as it is closely related to the similar distinction that used to be made between 'productive' and 'non-productive labour' and which is still followed in communist countries, i.e. production of physical commodities is 'productive'; of services, 'unproductive'.

In addition, this definition fitted in perfectly with the growth of the art of preparation of national accounts — it is in fact ideal for this. In the standard UN manual, *A System of National Accounts*, investment consists of fixed capital formation and increase in stocks and is measured by 'expenditures on tangible assets' (United Nations, 1968, p. 26). It should be noted here that this definition does not cover tangible assets owned by governments or by households except for homes. Nor does it cover intangible capital assets such as knowledge acquired through research owned by business firms or governments and skills and knowledge embodied in human beings that were acquired through training and education.

In recent years in the developed countries, after the focus of interest of some economists had shifted to longer-run problems of growth, the standard definition started to become less comfortable to live with. Since World War II, a number of studies in these countries appear to have found that economic growth has been greater than could be fully explained by growth in capital and labour. Some studies have in fact indicated that growth of the capital stock and labour force accounts for only a fraction of the total growth of gross national product (GNP) and that the 'unexplained residual factor' — accounts for as much as 50 – 85 per cent of total growth. Simon Kuznets has stated that while the results vary among individual countries, the inescapable conclusion is that growth in the labour force and capital accumulation account for scarcely more than a tenth of the rate of growth in per capita product. The rest must be assigned to an increase in efficiency due to the improved quality of the resources, the effects of changing arrangements, technological change, or to all of these (Kuznets, 1966, pp. 80 – 1).

Whether or not these studies are true for developed countries, in the developing countries it is clear that development depends on much more than material capital. At best, the provision of capital for material capital goods may account for about 50 per cent of economic growth in a developing country within the middle range of income. The economic analyses of developing countries prepared by World Bank country economic missions repeatedly bring out the importance of other factors. For example, Upper Volta's principal problem in economic development is the devastating effect of disease on agricultural productivity — malaria, bilharzia, river blindness and tuberculosis reduce the amount of labour available at times critical for growing crops (Kamarck, 1976, pp. 71 – 2). What this means is that, in Upper Volta, economic development at present is strongly dependent on health expenditures on medicine, other medical supplies, doctors, nurses and research. But health expenditures, except for a small amount for bricks and mortar and some medical equipment, in the conventional analysis are not classified as investment — they are current expenditures. Another example: cocoa is still the dominant element in Ghana's economy and the development of cocoa production is why Ghana used to have the second highest GNP per capita in tropical Africa. Of the total increase in capacity of

Ghana's cocoa trees between the 1950s and the 1960s of about 50 per cent, the development and use of insecticides, by increasing the survival rate of young trees, accounted for about one-third or 100,000 tons of the total annual output of cocoa. The rest were new plantings. Under the conventional definition of investment, the new plantings were investment; the expenditure on insecticides was not.

Technical assistance to the less developed countries is an exceedingly important integral part of almost all official development aid and its magnitude is consequently difficult to measure — it probably amounts to around 10 per cent of the total or around $3 billion a year. It has grown in response primarily to the actual experience of the needs of the developing countries. But where does it fit into present theory? For the OECD Development Assistance Committee countries, technical assistance is an important part of their 'Official Development Assistance'. In the balance of payments of the recipient country it shows up as a debit or receipt of services in the current account and as a credit or unrequited transfer in the transfers on capital account. In the national accounts of the recipient country it shows up not as investment but as consumption. (This might seem a good reason for taxpayers in developed countries to revolt — here is a clear case of economic aid financing 'consumption' in the developing countries. But, in fact, technical assistance is often among the most popular aid activities because, in spite of its economic classification, it is seen to be directly contributing to development.) The activities that are covered by technical assistance are not conventionally classed as 'investment' except for any expenditure on the incidental equipment involved. Any expenditure made by the recipient government on technical cooperation is a non-investment expenditure. It is a current expenditure of the government — that is to say, it is classed as the kind of expenditure that by the accepted theory should be held down in order to free funds so that 'savings' can be increased in order to finance investment in material capital.

Again, while it is highly likely that economic development in many countries could be speeded up if the rate of population growth declined, the bulk of expenditures on family planning programmes are classified as current expenditures and therefore 'bad', and not as investment which alone is seen to be 'good'.

The Green Revolution in agriculture that resulted in very large increases in output of wheat and rice in some developing countries was the outcome of expenditure of money that mostly went for salaries of research workers; only a small fraction was spent on what economists classify as investment, i.e. durable capital goods. In our conventional economic theory, only the expenditure on the buildings erected to house the research workers and any permanent improvement in the structure of the fields are classified as capital. The countries applying the discoveries of the Green Revolution increase expenditure on agricultural extension agents (i.e. 'current inputs'), on fertilizers, on pesticides, on improved seeds. When output goes up by 300 or 500 per cent, under our conventional theory suddenly it is the material capital goods that have become more productive. Through the capital – output ratio, this auxiliary or secondary expenditure is given the credit for the increase in agricultural output, whereas everyone knows that what really counted was the research brains that were applied to the problem.

The difficulty is primarily that investment is defined as 'expenditure on durable goods', whereas the most useful definition would appear to be 'expenditure that results in a flow of future income'. The product of such investment is capital. Such a definition has good, solid theoretical foundation for it. It is essentially based on the definition worked out by some of the founding fathers of modern economics who worked mostly on capital theory.

With the principal problem in developed countries up to World War II that of full employment, and with the growth of systems of national accounts as a policy tool to help guide the necessary policies, restricting the definition of investment to expenditure on durable capital goods was more practicable and sufficiently met the needs of economic policy in the developed countries. But even the argument that this definition is consistent with actual business practice is now weakened. Where is the real investment in IBM — in the fixed capital of its factories or in its organizations of able and talented people? In the important new high technology industries the lesser importance of durable goods is even more evident. The management of National Semiconductor warned off potential corporate raiders in 1977 by announcing that in the event of an adverse take-over the company would follow a 'scorched-earth' policy. It did not mean that it would destroy the buildings and equipment; these would be left intact for the new owners. It meant rather that the management and key technologists would resign *en masse* and thus leave the company an empty shell in economic reality. The recovery of Germany (West and East) and Japan after World War II showed that the most important part of the capital of these countries was not in the material capital goods that had been destroyed but in their trained people. The East German example is particularly striking; not only did the country not receive foreign aid, but much of the undestroyed capital equipment was removed as reparations to the Soviet Union.

As we have seen, even in the more developed countries, as the major policy interests shifted away from control of the cycle to growth or to the elimination of poverty pockets, economists began to find the existing definition crippling. Consequently, some economists proposed classifying at least part of the expenditures on education as investment in human capital. H. G. Johnson proposed that we go back to the concept whereby investment would be defined to include increasing health, discipline, skill and education, moving labour into more productive occupations and locations, and applying new knowledge to increase the efficiency of productive processes (H. G. Johnson, 1964, p. 221). P. T. Bauer, B. S. Yamey (Bauer and Yamey, 1957), Joan Robinson (1965), Paul Streeten (1972) and other economists have made similar suggestions in the past. Theodore Morgan has proposed giving up the use of the terms 'investment' and 'consumption' in the design of development plans and economic policy and set up instead a hierarchy of uses for expenditures from those that give the highest returns to those that are lowest. Some conventional 'consumption' uses of resources may be at or near the peak (T. Morgan, 1969, p. 404). (While unorthodox and original, Morgan's approach shows that he understands that the richness of economic reality can be properly grasped and controlled only by the logic of loose concepts.)

In actual fact, when the World Bank makes a decision as to the economic worth of an individual project, the economic appraisal techniques applied are based essentially on the broader definition of investment suggested above and not on the material capital goods definition: in calculating the internal rate of return or the cost − benefit ratio of a project, the so-called 'current' and 'capital' expenditures are both included on the cost side and compared with the flow of benefits, with both sides of the accounts suitably discounted over time. The narrower definition of investment comes into play only after the project passes the economic test and a decision has to be made for determining the eligibility of particular expenditure items for Bank financing. Even so, a substantial percentage of total loan expenditures is on items that do not fit within the material capital goods category. But then when the Bank and the government pass to the national or macro-level, only the expenditure on material capital goods is included in the investment accounts.

In my view, it is now time for economists working on problems of developing countries to accept fully the Fisherian definition of investment: that investment is any outlay made today for the purpose of increasing future income — whatever the asset (tangible or intangible, a piece of machinery or a piece of productive knowledge, a passable road or a functioning family planning organization) that is purchased with the outlay (Fisher, 1927). A short-run investment is one that pays off in a short term; a long-term investment is one where the return comes in over a longer period. The whole apparatus of investment decision can be applied to this as it is applied now to the purchase of durable goods. The figures and calculations will be less precise but the analysis and conclusions will be more correct. Once this is accepted, a lot of the problems that have been bothering us will fall into place. The various subterfuges that people have had to adopt in recent years in trying to get around the existing theory will no longer be necessary.

So far, most of my remarks have applied mainly to the public sector and public investment policy. The conventional approach through government income tax policy may also distort private economic decisions in all countries. The taxable income of corporations has, of course, to be defined — and this means defining what is 'investment'. If investment is defined, as it usually is, as the purchase of durable capital goods, then only the annual tranche of depreciation can be deducted from the year's current gross receipts in the process of ascertaining what is the taxable income. But if a capital expenditure is any outlay today that increases future income, it is clear that some of the most important business investment is not in material capital goods but in research and development, training of technical, scientific and managerial employees, learning by doing, and advertising (Vernon Smith, 1970, p. 29). All these categories of investment are fully expensed for corporate income tax purposes and are thereby given a subsidy of nearly 50 per cent in the United States, for example, by comparison with investment in hardware. The economic consequences are that the present tax depreciation laws are not likely to have the same effect on a railway or steel manufacturer that they have on a pharmaceutical, cigarette or management consulting firm whose investment in knowledge (including advertising) may be more important than their expenditures for hardware.

The impact of the argument in this chapter on the theme of this book is that economists need to shift from the conventional industrialized country concepts of capital and investment, which are easier to measure, to concepts that are harder to measure precisely but are more relevant. As the old basic fixed capital-intensive industries, such as iron and steel, are shrinking while the new high technology 'knowledge' industries are growing, the old concepts are increasingly misleading in policy-making. As mentioned in chapter 7, in many countries investment estimates are compiled by taking trade figures on imports of equipment and machinery and adding to them estimates of construction, or simply applying a factor to them. Under the proposed definition, investment would be considerably harder to estimate and the estimates would be even rougher and more imprecise. But the estimates would be more meaningful in relating investment to development and in providing a guide to policy.

If economic theory is to be really useful in guiding the developing countries to make good development plans, the 'capital goods = capital' confusion should be eliminated once and for all. This should also help to eliminate the gulf that has developed in recent years in development economics between those economists and econometricians, on the one hand, who regard quantification of economics so important that they insist on trying to quantify even though what they turn out may prove irrelevant for policy, and those economists who, living with day-to-day problems of economic development, find the existing theory irrelevant and so resort to 'judgement', intuition, or other essentially non-objective factors. The new (or rather older) definitions of capital and investment in developing countries will put investment back into the centre of development as the driving force. It should make decision-making a more rational process again.

The present situation, in which economists spend their time measuring what is easy to measure (durable capital goods) instead of trying to measure what is less precise but what really matters, is like the story of the drunk who had lost some money. He hunted for it under a street light because the light was better, rather than looking for it in the dark alley where he had really lost it. If economists truly want to be useful, we have to look where the problems are, and not where it is easiest to look.

11

Operational Conclusions

The process *is* the reality.

Alfred N. Whitehead, *Process and Reality*

The only solid piece of scientific truth is that we are profoundly ignorant about nature. Indeed, I regard this as the major discovery of the past hundred years of biology.

Lewis Thomas, *The Medusa and the Snail*

The implications of the foregoing chapters are definitely disquieting and hard to accept. The argument leads to the conclusion that the margins of precision in economics become increasingly wider as more sectors are covered, or as the subject matter becomes more complicated through involving more and more 'loose' concepts in a single logical argument, or as provision for time elapsing in a sequential decision problem or analysis has to cope with change over time in the real meaning of the concepts (variables, parameters, structure) involved. This is psychologically difficult to accept because we take precision to be synonymous with certainty and like all people we have a thirst for certainty. What the argument of this book demands, instead, is what John Keats called the high quality of 'negative capability'. That is, in economics we must have the courage and the capability to accept the need to operate with the uncertainties and doubts of the real world without any 'irritable reaching' for the security blanket of unwarranted and unattainable precision and without turning our backs on real problems simply because they cannot be grasped by precise mathematical models.

The operational conclusions that flow from this approach should come easier to economists whose view of economic reality is that of a continuing dynamic process irreversible in time rather than that of a well-structured system that strongly tends towards a general equilibrium (see, for example, Schumpeter, 1949; Nelson and Winter, 1977; Georgescu-Roegen, 1971; Kaldor, 1972). This approach has some very broad implications. In this concluding chapter, we can cover only some of these, the ones that I regard as most important for applied economics and economic policy. The topics discussed fall into three groups: (a) the attitude towards economic data, (b) the implications for economic analysis, and (c) policy-making.

Economic data

Economic 'individuals' are not definite, economic classes are not exact and economic categories are not *sharp*. Therefore, economic data cannot be as precise as data in the physical sciences. The sources of economic data may have a conscious or unconscious interest in distorting them, hence the accuracy of data must always be examined by the test of *cui bono?* This does not mean that economists should throw up their hands and abandon attempts to use quantitative data. What it does mean is that economists should be aware of the degree of precision or of bias that the data they use may have. It means also that economists need to learn about how the degree of accuracy or precision in one component affects the whole. All too often an economist spends an enormous amount of effort in computing and manipulating data that have turned into 'noise' without the economist having become aware of it. The roughest element in a calculation decides the precision of the result (see the Technical Appendix on significant digits).

Except for economists who are primarily interested in constructing science fiction models about a non-existent reality, it is essential that anyone who works with economic data have some experience in the process of raw data gathering. For serious analysts, there must be clear specification of the data that are needed for the hypothesis or problem being considered, a thorough understanding of the data that exist or can be gathered and a careful weighing of the effects of the deviations between the data wanted and the actual data that can be used. Some perception is needed as to how the data are actually secured from the primary sources, of the possible margins of error involved because of the play of the various self-interests of the providers of data, and how close the proxy concepts are that are actually measured to those the economist really wants. Anyone who manipulates economic data without such knowledge is operating in the dark. Computations of sampling errors, sensitivity analyses, tests of significance and measures of dispersion are meaningless if one is not sure that the data used are even distantly related to what is supposedly being measured. The calculated regression line one is working with may not even be within the band that would truly bracket reality.

Economists need to work in the neglected field that Jack Triplett has called the 'economics of measurement' (1977, p. 140). That is, in each branch of economics it is necessary to do systematic work on using the concepts of economic theory to specify what we want to measure; to investigate how closely the existing measures correspond to the concepts of theory; to determine whether, how and to what extent the concepts are measurable in the real world; and to establish what the consequences are for the theory and for applied economics of the deviations between the measures that are or can be produced and what is required by existing theory. Because economists have done so little of this necessary groundwork and have appeared content to work with whatever figures are produced, governments have been allowed to neglect the provision of adequate resources to gather the economic statistics needed. Billions of dollars have been spent on space probes and to lift telescopes into earth orbit to improve astronomers' observations on rocks and gases in outer space while a comparatively miniscule pittance is spent to improve the quality and scope of the data on the economic system on which we all depend. Decisions are taken by governments and international organizations in allocating billions of dollars in economic aid and loans to less developed countries on the basis of figures produced by under-manned, poorly equipped, badly financed statistical offices and no urgency is shown in helping these countries to improve their data.

The improvement we are concerned with is mostly in the scope and accuracy of the data. Many statistics that already exist are precise; their drawback is that most are misleading. Precise data are not indispensable for analysis or policy-making. Merely knowing the probable direction of change is often important. Data do not have to be precise to make possible a prediction whether things will go up or down, whereas it is impossible to predict precisely how far or at what speed the change will occur. It may be vital to know whether some variable is likely to increase or decrease and whether the probable consequences are large or small, while the precise magnitude of the change is impossible to ascertain and not necessary for the decision. In sum, while it would be ideal always to be able to apply a quantitative calculus to economic analysis, when economic reality makes this impossible this does not mean that nothing can be done: a qualitative calculus is often useful and may even be sufficient.

One of the strong points of the 'new public finance' is that it recognizes the problem of taxation in a mixed economy as a problem of indirect control of *imperfectly observable variables*. One might like to have a tax on ability but one can observe only income, which is a compound of ability and effort; one might like to distinguish between wage and capital income in the self-employed sector but there is no obvious way to do so (Stiglitz and Boskin, 1977, p. 295).

Sets of independent rough data that reinforce each other provide more assurance than a single set of precise data that are suspect. National accounts in countries that compute a full set of income, product and expenditure accounts that interlock and verify each other provide considerable support for analysis. The recently developed new tool of country and regional economic analysis, the Social Accounting Matrix (SAM), is particularly valuable in this regard. It makes it possible to embody in a single articulated matrix the available information of a set of national accounts, a flow-of-funds table and an input – output table. It provides a logical framework to organize the available dispersed and fragmentary information about an economy. It makes the most of existing data, and its construction forces the economist to identify the gaps, discrepancies and inconsistencies in the figures. It provides clues as to the causes of discrepancies and focuses attention on where further work is most needed. It is, in short, a tool that recognizes and addresses the real problems of handling the inconsistent, unreliable and scanty data available on the economies of many countries. (For an able introduction to SAM, see King, 1981.)

It is well to keep in mind that there is a very high noise to signal ratio in any set of short-term economic data — in fact, at times, a disturbing statistic may be nothing but noise. Monthly figures on GNP, balance of payments, unemployment, etc. cannot be taken at face value. Quarterly figures are only somewhat better. In all cases, to be credible, any sudden change in any series should be substantiated by evidence from other independent sources. To find out what is going on in the economy and as a check on official statistics, empirical economists learn to value information drawn directly from economic life, such as surveys of consumer attitudes and business sentiments and reports from purchasing agents of corporations on new orders, prices, inventories. For the longer term, for example in evaluating the longer-term economic prospects of countries, economic statistics provide only the starting point. The decisive factors in determining the future include such items as non-quantifiable capability of the major interest groups to work together, the ease of upward mobility for people of talent, the openness of economic leaders to innovation, the ability of the people to adapt to new circumstances and to rise to challenges. In working on economic problems, economists cannot be effective if they insist on wearing blinkers and excluding all economic information that is not presented in numbers.

It will be recalled that the great mathematician Gauss stated that a lack of mathematical learning is revealed by unlimited precision in computations. Most people unfortunately do basically lack mathematical learning — even some of those who nimbly manipulate numbers and symbols — and are only favourably impressed by a string of figures given to one or two decimal places. Economists, no matter how quantitative, who are basically ignorant of mathematics or who are cynical practitioners of what Ely Devons (1961) called 'statistical magic' rather than statistical analysis will not wish to recognize the inherent lack of precision in economic data. The rest of us can only be helped by the perception that going beyond the possible margins of precision involves us in nothing but the manipulation of noise and in self-deception. Historians, after a brief quantitative fling, have apparently learned this lesson faster than economists. Perhaps this is because historians, like the natural scientists but unlike economists, are trained in the harsh discipline of basing their analyses on personal involvement in systematic fact-finding. The historian Lawrence Stone has described their present approach: most historians count today but only when it seems appropriate and they keep in mind the strictly limited potential for manipulating such imprecise data as historical evidence is (Lawrence Stone, 1979, p. 21).

An economist must have the courage to recognize frankly and to describe honestly the quality of the data he is working with. The proper perception of the roughness and inexactness of the data is an essential part of developing the informed judgement that is basic for good economic analysis. The knowledge that an economist cannot blindly manipulate numbers leads to the need to develop an intuitive feeling of the proper orders of magnitude of the data being worked with. The economist must also have a basic concern for integrating theoretical analysis with the data of the real world. He must know how the phenomenon he is concerned with has behaved in the past, how it fits into the economy, what the major forces are that impinge on it, how other statistics are supposed to mesh with the series he is working with. With these basic ingredients of informed judgement, the economist is better able, for example, to evaluate the likelihood that what his figures show truly represents what is happening or is merely a statistical aberration. Robert Dorfman presents an example to emulate. In commenting on some research results, he states '. . . we do not regard the computations as having any high degree of reliability. They are perhaps suggestive but certainly untrustworthy' (Dorfman, 1977, p. 336).

Economic analysis

In the discussion, we have already had to touch on some of the implications of this exposition on the approach to economic analysis and policy-making. In the main, the conclusions confirm what successful economic policy-makers usually have learned through experience. In the quotation that began this book, Koopmans states his belief that economics as a practical art is ahead of economics as a science. I agree with Koopmans' conclusion, but what it also means is that something is wrong or missing in the usual approach to economics as a science. If we accept that economics is about economic reality and we recognize the limitations imposed by reality on what economics can do, then there should be no striking constrast between economics as 'art' (i.e. economics applied to analysis of real problems) and economics as 'science' (i.e. a body of theories about the real world that have met the test of empirical observations). Economic science is applied and advanced by economist-practitioners who struggle with the economic models of the real world and not by those economists who live prestigious and happy lives playing with 'elegant models of comely shape but without vital organs'. The lessons taught by economic reality are good economic theory.

The illusion that a science of economics is different in kind from economics as an empirical art has led much of economics into a sterile wasteland. The economic journals indicate that many of the most prestigious academic economists are working on theoretical mathematical models that begin with entirely arbitrary and mostly unrealistic assumptions and lead to precisely stated and irrelevant conclusions as far as the real world is concerned. Of the articles published in the *American Economic Review* (the journal of the American Economic Association) from 1972 to 1981, over half were on mathematical models without any data. Only 1 per cent were empirical analyses based on data that had been researched by the author himself (Leontief, 1982). It is not surprising, consequently, that there has been so little progress in recent years in advancing our knowledge and ability to cope with the problems of the economic system. When President Carter at mid-term tried to carry out a reassessment of the position of the United States through meeting with a sample of people from all fields, he reported bitterly that his meeting with economists was a waste of time: the economists seemed unwilling or unable 'to deal in a practical way with the economic problems I was having to face every day'.

The drift in economics away from consideration of real problems towards scholasticism is apparently an almost irresistible temptation in academia in all subjects. Career pressures 'to publish or to perish' encourage work on articles that emphasize technical sophistication of technique rather than time-consuming laborious work on real-world problems. In philosophy, Karl Popper has warned that genuine philosophy is rooted in serious problems. Philosophers who are not concerned with such problems but produce exercises in fashionable methods lure philosophy into 'the bog of pseudo-problems and verbal puzzles' (Popper, 1964, p. 72). Even in such an empirical subject as engineering is, there has been a trend that parallels economics in painful detail. As Paul Liber describes it, in the engineering schools there are influential groups whose main interest is not in actual problems but in the investigation of mathematical models under boundary conditions that can be conveniently handled. This leads easily to a high rate of publication. Being formal and logical, model-building is easy to organize and to lecture on, and confers great prestige. It often attracts the better students and through them is propagated. Unfortunately, it is 'virtually ineffective' in creating new technology (Liber, 1962, pp. 8 – 9).

If economics is to be a true science and deal with problems of the world of reality, it has to begin with a proper appreciation of what economic measurements can and cannot do. In economics we must deal with loose concepts. In handling loose concepts the margins of precision of a statistic must widen as it slips away from describing or measuring the central area of the concept (where theoretically it can be sharp or precise) towards the grey area or penumbra in which most of the real world concepts live. In physics, it is possible to assume that the formal properties of the mathematical symbols are isomorphous with the empirical relations of the categories they represent in the real world. Since the mathematical language of the theory can be taken to mirror reality correctly, mathematical manipulation of the model results in quite specific predictions whose precise confirmation from reality then validates the whole chain of manipulation (Zinman, 1978, pp. 163 – 4). In economics, this isomorphism, this *precise* identity of symbols and reality, does not exist.

Once one accepts that the particular set of data one is working with is not very accurate, that only the first or second digits are significant and that the categories or concepts that are being measured are themselves loose and not sharp, then it follows that one cannot manipulate these mechanically in carrying out analysis or in determining policy. Only in economic problems that are narrowly limited, with relatively sharp categories and fairly precise and accurate data, can one rely on a model to *determine* a solution. In most cases, the economist must, to a smaller or greater degree, apply his experience, his knowledge of other facts (quantitative or non-quantitative); in brief, he must use his judgement to interpret and to modify the results from his model.

It is necessary to recognize that often the closest that economics can come to portraying some reality is in the form of a rough, simple model. These models need to be considered not as algorithms or effective procedures providing us with precise solutions to economic problems but rather as heuristics. That is, they are plausible approaches or rules of thumb for attacking particular problems or for illuminating some particular aspect of the structure of reality. They may give us reasonable approximate solutions with reasonable amounts of computation. They cannot dictate or determine the precise single right decision, but should rather assist us in making rational and effective decisions.

As the scope of an economic problem or model is widened by 'chunking' an increasing portion of an economy or is extended by covering a longer time period, it necessarily becomes increasingly less precise. (It also becomes increasingly subject to exogenous influences that may not be quantifiable at all but that, if sufficiently important, must be taken account of.) The application of the technique of significant digits in this process will result in the dropping of narrow parameters and, perhaps, the replacement of a whole set by a single broad class parameter. Paradoxically, as the scope of a model widens or extends, it correspondingly must become simpler or rougher, since more detailed and more precise numbers will reproduce only more noise. An aggregate model of the whole economy can be, at best, only a 'sketch' or 'construct'.

As economic models move beyond the attempt to grasp more than a very simple, accurately measurable bit of reality, they become less and less isomorphic to reality. There is less and less precision in the mapping of the structural relations of reality onto the model. It may even happen that the economist may need the 'negative capability' to conclude that no quantitative model or formula is sufficiently good to rely on and the only recourse is to rely on informed judgement. The National Bureau of Economic Research made just such a courageous decision in its consideration of whether or not it could establish some kind of objective quantitative formula by which the development of a recession in the economy could be recognized. The Bureau decided it could not do so. Its reasoning is consistent with the argument of this book. The Bureau concluded that recessions are infrequent compared to the rate of change in the structure of the economy so any formula would have to be modified at least as often as a recession occurs. We are unable to forecast the nature of the shocks that drive the economy into a recession: a formula set up before 1973 would not have worked to establish the turning points in 1973 and 1975. The basic data are government data and their conceptual basis and statistical behaviour change from time to time. Consequently, the NBER concluded, '. . . for this issue there is no substitute for informed judgment' (Hall, 1979, p. 144).

A real-world problem never has its individuals completely definite, its classes exact, its boundaries sharp, its rules well defined and clear cut, and it is never sealed off from any other part of the world with absolute certainty. Consequently, deductive mathematical reasoning alone can no longer be regarded as sufficient to reach satisfactory answers. The economist must supplement deductive reasoning by calling on his faculties for reasoning by analogy and on his intuition, insight and judgement that have come from his distillation of rich experience. The research on artificial intelligence has shown that processes that carry out deductive reasoning can be programmed on essentially one level. But real intelligence has been found to be much more comprehensive and multi-level. It has an overview capacity: rather than remaining confined in a fixed mechanical framework, it has an ability to jump out of the system, to see analogies in deeply related ideas that appear unrelated. In brief, my argument is that, as economists, we should not limit the use of our minds to the single level of deductive reasoning but should use the full range of our intelligence (see also Lawson, 1981).

Policy-making

For handling managerial problems within a firm when the objective can be simply defined (minimize costs of holding inventory, minimize cash holdings, pick the area to drill for oil where the expected return is greatest, for example), there has been a considerable development of useful decision techniques. These include linear programming, operations research and management science. Even here, it is easy to find practical problems where exact and timely solutions are beyond the present and prospective computational resources. Recourse has to be made to heuristic procedures that may help to give reasonable approximate solutions with reasonable amounts of computation (or to rules of thumb that may help in but do not guarantee finding a solution). This is to be contrasted with effective procedures or algorithms that are guaranteed when applied to find exact solutions sooner or later. H. A. Simon (1978) points out that the fact that an algorithm exists that makes possible an exact solution is not helpful if the time required is not justified for the problem involved. Some classes of problems are 'exponential' — that is, as we increase the number of problem elements, the maximum time required for solution rises exponentially. But for some of these, the time required for solution can be reduced if we are willing to settle for approximate solutions. For more complex problems arising from uncertain situations with high probability of error and surprise (what Russell Stout calls 'development problems'), successful managers use a strategy of acting incrementally and redundantly, to preserve the chance to learn as action proceeds and to guard against excessive costs from errors (Stout, 1980, p. 151).

For the area we are mostly concerned with — that is, economic policy-making by governments — the problems are even more complex. Formally, a decision problem can be broken down into four elements: (1) an objective function, which states the objective to be maximized or minimized (the dependent variable); (2) the range of policy alternatives or instruments of policy (the independent policy or decision variables) among which the decision-maker can choose in accordance with his desire to achieve the objective; (3) the model that specifies the structure or the empirical relations connecting the instruments, the variables entering the objective function and other relevant variables; (4) the computational procedures by which the government, through the model, finds the values of the instruments that will optimize the objective function (Arrow, 1957). As I have tried to show in the discussion throughout the book, every aspect of this formal model can apply only roughly when it must be used in the real world. Except in very restricted managerial problems, it is generally impossible to specify precisely an objective function in governmental policy; the policy instruments are not independent but are intertwined with the objectives; the structural equations are not known with great accuracy or precision; or there is no practicable algorithm that would yield an exact solution in any responsible span of time or at any reasonable cost.

Since we cannot grasp an economy in a highly precise model, we cannot control precisely (or 'fine-tune') the course of an economy. With all its centralized planning experience of over six decades and a pervasive secret police, the USSR has not been able to make the actual outcomes exactly match its plans. In the more decentralized economies, we must recognize that economic policy cannot exactly *determine* the course of the economy. Policy-making must start, therefore, with realistic expectations of results.

One consequence is that there is a strong case when new decisions have to be made in a largely unknown problem area for the policy approach of incrementalism or 'muddling through'. If you find yourself in a completely dark strong room and must try to find your way through, you do so by making small groping steps, changing direction as you bump into obstacles. In public policy, the actual problems are more complex because there are nearly always several rather than just one objective involved — you not only have to get through the dark room, you have to locate and carry out a heavy chest without waking the inhabitants.

As Lindblom has shown, further, objectives and policies are intertwined and the choice among policies means choosing how much more of one objective one wants as against another (Lindblom, 1959). For example (changing the metaphor to a more realistic instance), a government in a less developed country wants to increase agricultural output and also wants to break up the large estates to get a more even distribution of income and power in the countryside. Confiscation and distribution of the large farms will achieve the second objective but will reduce agricultural output and create a balance of payments crisis. If it is politically feasible to proceed more cautiously, the policy-maker in these circumstances may find it wiser to weigh the different alternatives at the margin (as a well-brought-up economist should) and to start by imposing a moderately progressive land tax on large estates to finance a programme of estate purchases and of equipping small farmers with necessary capital equipment. Then, as experience dictates, the next steps can be taken.

This approach is not a prescription for immobility. Effective policy-making has to accept the imprecision of knowledge of the present economic structure and the uncertainty of the future. The world is not all order, but neither is it all chaos. We are not completely ignorant of the present nor completely uncertain of the future. We do have a substantial, even if not very precise or very accurate, knowledge of the present, and we can ascertain most of the major trends presently at work that are shaping the future, as well as forecast within broad limits most of the probable range of major events that will affect the future. But the remaining developments that we cannot predict, the changes in the trends themselves or in the speed of their realization, are so important that we need to take these uncertainties into account in our policy-making.

From my own experience, I find the sailing metaphor most natural here. Economic analysis can provide a rough compass indicating the direction we want to go, but the seas of the future are largely uncharted and the winds and currents are unpredictable, so we have to realize that tacking will be inevitable if we wish to progress towards a given objective. The approach required, then, is to emphasize the development of policy strategy. Instead of calculating or working out a plan of action calling for a single unique line of implementation, it is better to work out a strategy that has rules for choosing future actions in response to later information — which cannot now be predicted sufficiently accurately. Sherman Maisel summarizes the lessons of his experience as a governor of the Federal Reserve Board in this way: 'Given the high risks of playing against nature, we may be far better off minimizing our costs by developing better control and feedback systems rather than trying to improve systems which will be efficient only if the forecasts are completely correct' (Maisel, 1974, p. 321).

For example, policy decisions to solve the energy problem the world confronts should not attempt to work out one single plan of action. No one knows how much oil and gas there still is to be discovered or when or at what cost it will be discovered and exploited. No one knows what processes will be invented to use economically the enormous oil reserves locked up in the oil shales and oil sands; or how, when and at what cost large-scale solar power electric cells will become economically feasible; or whether and how hydrogen can be produced to be an economic substitute for petrol as a fuel for cars. No one can predict except within very large margins what energy demand is going to be. In 1972, the US National Petroleum Council estimated that world petroleum demand in 1981 would be 76 million barrels a day; it turned out to be less than 47 million barrels a day. In 1978, projections made just three years into the future for US oil imports in 1981 were drastically wrong: projected, 11 million barrels a day; actual, 5.7 million (McKinley, 1982, pp. 1 – 2).

Rational decision-making requires that any plans worked out should take into account the high degree of ignorance about the variables and parameters and also the high probability of surprise — favourable and unfavourable. We have already learned that the price elasticity of demand for oil is higher than had been calculated. It will be necessary to take advantage of unexpected favourable winds and currents and to minimize the drift when winds and currents are adverse. Reserves need to be provided, and flexibility and even a measure of redundancy are positive virtues.

The future is unpredictable not only because future developments in technology and political changes may be unexpected but also because we change ourselves. In the course of carrying out plans that change our environment, we may ourselves acquire changed desires and interests and new objectives. Large-scale irreversible investment decisions that foreclose future options, even if successful in relation to initial objectives, may be disastrous to ultimate goals when completed. A city that bulldozes a system of freeways through its centre may find on completion that it has destroyed itself as a living civilized community.

In developing countries or regions, this analysis supports the importance of emphasizing the planning *process* rather than the mere preparation and execution of fixed development plans. It is more important to build an organization that gathers and analyses data, that helps the government to coordinate and to rationalize its economic and financial policies, that works to secure changes in government and private investment and operating decisions in accordance with changes in the economy and in line with new opportunities opening up than it is to prepare a formal multi-year development plan that invariably proves to be irrelevant soon after its completion. If personnel resources are available to do more and to prepare a formal plan in addition to providing analyses for the planning process, the plan should be a 'rolling' plan, i.e. one that is revised annually in the light of new developments. It should also provide for generous contingency reserves for emergencies and to exploit changed opportunity sets. Another means of increasing flexibility is to recognize that diversification has positive advantages over reliance on a single major product, a single market or a single supplier.

Trying to find solutions that will be relatively efficient even if rough is far better than deluding ourselves we can find the precisely correct answer to a problem and consequently neglecting what can be done. Once the search for a precise decision-making model as a solution to a particular policy problem is realized to be futile, alternative ways of mobilizing the knowledge, experience and judgement of policy-makers can be pursued. Among those that have proved effective are the techniques of the working party and the so-called Delphi technique. The working party, composed of the most expert and experienced people available on a particular problem, is given the task of producing a factual analysis of the important aspects of the problem and of the policy alternatives to be presented to the ultimate decision-makers. Through discussion and common analysis, the working party can usually arrive at a consensus that the members recognize as a better and more creative result than any one individual, with only his particular experience and judgement, could attain alone. The success of the Marshall Plan — an unprecedented, completely novel effort to aid the reconstruction of war-devastated Europe, initially working with highly dubious data — owes much to the working parties in the US government that put together the aid programme and the accompanying financial and economic policies.

The Delphi technique is a way of tapping the experience and judgement of a wide circle of people. Instead of working in a meeting, questionnaires on a particular policy problem are circulated to individuals who have some knowledge or talent to contribute. Each person writes his answers and sends them back. Then the answers are circulated to each of the members and they reconsider their original answers in the light of the others' remarks. Three cycles are usually enough; by that time, as much of a consensus has been developed as is possible.

A variant of the Delphi technique is also being used with some success. This approach organizes the assessment of probable outcomes by the most knowledgeable people concerned. When a decision is to be made, the experts on the different factors that could affect the outcome make informed estimates of the probabilities of relevant developments in their field. Based on these probabilities, a judgement is then reached.

It is a pity that the nature of economics and of economic reality is such that we cannot provide firm and sweeping guidelines to policy-making or develop sure-fire techniques or models that could be applied to policy problems and give deterministic definitive solutions. But we must recognize frankly the limitations of economics. Paraphrasing what Paul A. Samuelson said almost as an aside in his American Economic Association presidential address (1962), we must accept that ours is an uncertain truth and economists should be humble about its precision. But our humility should be based on our knowledge of the limitations of economics and not on our ignorance of them.

Paradoxically, the very recognition of the limitations of economics — its wide margins of precision — frees economists to a broader usefulness in policy-making. Once it is accepted that we are faced with a changing complex structure of reality that we can know only roughly, the policy field becomes wider. Usually policy decision-making is taken to be constricted to trying to select the most rational among the alternatives open within the field of choice that is bounded by the parameters that govern it. But if we realize that we can know the alternatives and parameters only roughly, we can find it easier to step outside the problem and to consider, first, whether we want to choose to accept or to try to change the parameters. For example, once we accept the fact that a Pareto-optimal decision (i.e. no one is worse off but at least one person is better off) cannot be precisely and accurately arrived at in a particular situation, we must realize that a specific decision is likely to result in some loss to some holders of property-rights as well as some gain to others. Taking a decision means, therefore, that one must consider whether the existing structure of rights is optimum or whether changes should be made. We find it easier, then, to realize that accepting Pareto-optimality as a valid goal means accepting the existing structure of rights as optimum. Pareto-optimality is not a value-free position, as it is often considered, but rather is a position that has an undeclared antecedent normative premise embedded in it — and this needs to be taken into account in making policy decisions (Samuels, 1978).

In many instances, it is necessary to recognize that the best representation of economic reality may be to calculate trends or tendencies or a particular pattern and to recognize these as such. The model will then clearly indicate to all who use it that there is nothing mechanically inevitable about the future in this particular aspect of economic reality — that, in fact, the crucial element may be merely a temporary constancy. (The best model possible in a particular case may be a statement of a tendency with a subjective probability distribution, based on the best available data and experience, to explain the likelihood of the model's approximating reality in the present — or in the future.) Because in many (if not most) cases, the data can only roughly measure reality, it is necessary to realize that often only relatively large changes or relatively large differences in comparative aggregates can be recognized as significant. For example, even if only roughly accurate, the national accounts can give a useful picture of the interrelations of the main aggregates and of major change in the economy.

Once we realize and take into account that the numbers we use do not accurately represent or precisely measure the categories they purport to correspond to in the real world, our policy decisions will be better. We will not give final weight to any series of numbers but seek to check them against other independent sources. Direct reports from economic factors may often give a better feel of where the economy is and is going than statistics processed with a delay through government offices. Polls of consumers and reports from purchasing managers of corporations have proved their worth in forecasting, for instance. While people immersed in an industry may seldom have a broad view of national problems, their knowledge of their own sector will usually surpass what can be derived from official statistics. Peter Drucker has properly chided economists for going too far away from experience, for moving from abstraction to abstraction without touching the solid ground of reality. While experience without the test of logic is mere 'chitchat', logic without the test of experience is absurdity (Drucker, 1979, p. 203).

Finally, all this underlines the importance of informed judgement, based on rich experience and theory, in policy-making. In physics, the working out of an appropriate model, which is isomorphic to the reality concerned, provides the solution to a problem in the real world. In economics, every responsible economist and econometrician would agree that an econometric model is no substitute for good judgement — at best a model identifies the factors on which judgement must be brought to bear. But judgement is not something that can be quantified and measured *ex ante*. It is, in short, the final aspect of economic analysis and policy-making that defies accurate categorization and precise measurement even though we can learn from experience who has or does not have good economic judgement.

The economic policies of the industrialized world in the last decade have not met with brilliant success. However, in comparison to the disastrous period after World War I, it is undeniable that, the record since World War II, influenced by the advances in economic knowledge, has been immeasurably superior. The economic difficulties of the present are probably due more to the prevalent scholasticism that diverts many of the most brilliant of the profession away from work on real problems than we are willing to admit. It is equally undeniable that the pace of economic development in the less developed countries in the last 30 years, while uneven, has been more rapid and widespread than ever in history. Further, the one explanatory factor that appears to hold true in accounting for the greater success of some less developed countries as compared to others in similar circumstances is that the more successful countries are those that have had able, pragmatic economic management. In sum, rough as it must be, economic knowledge can be effective in producing desired policy results.

As a quotation from Aristotle introduced this book, it may appropriately be concluded with the sage philosophy of the first great economist on how a subject like economics should be approached:

> In studying this subject we must be content if we attain as high a degree of certainty as the matter of it admits. . . . Such being the nature of our subject and such our way of arguing in our discussions of it, we must be satisfied with a rough outline of the truth, and for the same reason we must be content with broad conclusions. (*Nicomachean Ethics*)

Technical Appendix
Significant Digits

'Significant digits' is a basic scientific technique, ignored by economists, of presenting quantitative data that conveys exactly the degree of precision to be ascribed to the numbers. In physics, even though physical quantities or relationships can be much more accurately measured than most economic quantities, physicists are taught from the beginning the need to be aware of the margins of error and to cope with them through the technique of manipulation of 'significant digits'. This is not a complicated technique, but it is essential to the understanding of what a number means and to a more accurate manipulation of numbers.

'Significant digits' is the simple alternative to (1) stating numbers with the quantification of margin of error, i.e. stating an output estimate, for example, as $a \pm e$, or (2) stating numbers with their probability density function, i.e. stating a price forecast, for example, where the range is from a to b $[a \leqslant p \leqslant b]$ as $\int_{a}^{b} f(p) \, dp = 1$. Using probability density functions is by far the most accurate way of conveying the information in an economic estimate or measurement, but it is also, even with computers, largely unmanageable for most uses. The significant digit technique can, as I shall try to show below, make probability analysis somewhat more simple.

Specifying the margin of error can also be more accurate than significant digits since significant digits is essentially formalizing a statement of margin of error within the last decimal place. But if there is much numerical computation involved in an analysis, manipulation of numbers with specified margins of error becomes extremely awkward and cumbersome. It is largely for such reasons that the physical sciences have adopted significant digits as the convention to be used. The significant digit technique furnishes a decision rule as to how much precision a number is meant to represent. And, as the great mathematician Gauss stated, control over the extent of precision in mathematical computations is one of the tests by which real mathematical understanding is evidenced.

The fundamental point is to recall what the meaning of a number is when used in measurement in the real world rather than in 'pure' theory. A number, 14 for example, is said to have two significant digits, which means that the number of tens is known exactly and the last digit (the number of units in this case) has been rounded and is not precise. (If we knew the number of units exactly, the number would be written as 14.0; that is, with three significant digits.) This number's 'possible error' (i.e. its greatest variation up or down) is 0.5. So '14' means 14 ± a possible error of 0.5; that is, the true quantity is somewhere between 14.5 and 13.5. The final bit of relevant information conveyed is that the 'relative error' in the figure 14 *is* 4 per cent.
$$\frac{0.5}{14} \times 100$$

The significant digits rules apply to the *non-zero* digits to the left of the decimal point (and to all digits to the right of the decimal point). That is, the number 6000 means the true value lies between 5500 and 6500; 6200 means the true value lies between 6150 and 6250; 6240 means the true value lies between 6235 and 6245; 6243 means the true value lies between 6242.5 and 6243.5. If, in fact, we are sure through the tens place in the number 6000, we can write it $60\overline{0}0$ or $600\dot{0}$, with a bar or a dot over the final zero to indicate that it is significant. A better technique is to use scientific notation, in which the significant digits are those given in the mantissa; e.g. the foregoing numbers would be written as 6×10^3 (if we are really sure of the tens place: 6.000×10^3), 6.2×10^3, 6.24×10^3, and 6.243×10^3.

The bit of information conveyed in the 'number of significant digits' in a quantity makes it possible for us to apply a simple rule to determine how accurate our answer can be in any mathematical operation. It can provide a guide to how much actual information is being conveyed by a number and how much of it is just noise. It can provide a guide to how much precision is warranted and how much is, at best, waste motion and, at worst, plain misleading.

Multiplication, division, roots

In the operations of multiplication, division, roots, the answer is accurate to a number of significant digits no greater and usually less than the number of significant digits in *any one* of the original numbers. That is to say, the answer can be accurate only so far as the accuracy of the *least* accurate number. Like a chain, it can be no stronger than its weakest link. Just as it is useless waste to strengthen all other links of the chain and leave one weak, so it is useless and misleading to manipulate data to a large number of places when one item is known only very roughly.

If, for example, we multiply 141 by 17, we are multiplying one number with three significant digits by another with two significant digits. The answer, then, can have at most two significant digits. According to arithmetic, the two pure numbers 141 times 17 equal 2397. But in measuring the real world, the last two digits in this answer, are only 'noise' and there may also be doubt about the third digit. Multiplying 141 by 17 means multiplying 141 ± 0.5 by 17 ± 0.5, which gives a range for the answer of 2318.25 to 2476.25. In other words, we are reasonably certain that the correct answer is closer to 2000 than to 1000 or 3000. We can be only reasonably certain that our answer is safe to one less significant digit than the number of significant digits in the least accurate figure being multiplied. We are fairly sure that it is closer to 2400 than to 2300 or 2500 (but it is possible that it could be either). We have no confidence at all that it is closer to 2400 than to 2390 or 2410.

The possible error in 141 as we defined it above is 0.5; in 17 it is also 0.5. In the product, if we accept 2400 as our figure, it is 80. This is a graphic example of how small errors magnify in the course of even simple calculations. The 'relative errors' in the two figures in our example were:

$$\frac{0.5}{141} \times 100 = 0.4 \text{ per cent}$$

$$\frac{0.5}{17} \times 100 = 3.0 \text{ per cent}$$

The relative error in our answer is:

$$\frac{80}{2400} \times 100 = 3.3 \text{ per cent}$$

that is, the relative error of the product is roughly the *sum* of the relative errors of the numbers multiplied.

The same principle holds for division; that is, if the smaller number of significant digits in either figure is n, the answer cannot have more than n significant digits, and one usually cannot rely that more than $(n - 1)$ of the digits are significant. The relative error of the quotient is also again roughly the sum of the relative errors of the component figures.

Addition and subtraction

In addition and subtraction, the approach has to be somewhat different. If we wish to add, say, 141 plus 5, both are accurate to the nearest unit, although the first has three significant digits and the second only one. That is, 141 ± 0.5 plus 5 ± 0.5 equals 146 ± 1. The answer, 146, then is accurate two significant digits and the third digit cannot be far off even though one of the addends has only one significant digit.

In adding (and subtracting) what matters is not the number of significant digits but *how far to the right the digits are significant. The sum (or difference) cannot be more accurate further to the right than any one of the addends.*

For example, the sums of the following two lists of figures must be the same, 2600, with the answer accurate in the thousands place and with the hundreds place only roughly correct.

2500	2500
110	120
18	22
4	3
2632 or 2600	2645 or 2600

If the sums are presented as 2632 or 2645, the last two digits, in this case 32 or 45, are just noise. This conclusion becomes obvious if one lists the figures with their errors. The first becomes:

$$2500 \pm 50$$
$$110 \pm 5$$
$$18 \pm 0.5$$
$$4 \pm 0.5$$
$$2632 \pm 56, \text{ or the underlying correct figure}$$
$$\text{is in the range of 2576 to 2688}$$

and the second:

$$2500 \pm 50$$
$$120 \pm 5$$
$$22 \pm 0.5$$
$$\underline{3 \pm 0.5}$$

2645 ± 56, or the underlying correct figure
is in the range of 2589 to 2701

These examples also make it clear that it is a waste of time to attempt to get any of the numbers that are going to be summed more accurate than one more place to the right than the least accurate addend. That is, the example given here (2500) has significant digits only to the hundreds place, therefore the cost-effective procedure is not to waste time trying to get the other figures more accurate than the tens place. The summations should then have been:

2500	2500
110	120
20	20
0	0
2630, rounded to 2600	2640, rounded to 2600

The examples also showed that the error in the sum (or difference) of several numbers is equal to the total of the errors.

The relative error in the sum is heavily influenced by the relative error of the largest addend. In the first example, the relative errors are as follows:

	Relative errors (%)
2500	2
110	5
18	3
4	13
2632	2

To summarize, the number of significant digits (or the degree of precision) of the basic data governs how accurate the final answer can be in any mathematical operation; it also governs the extent to which sophisticated or refined treatment of the data is valid — beyond this it becomes wasteful, misleading or self-deceptive.

Sensitivity analysis

Sensitivity analysis, which is widely used by economists, is not a substitute for the use of significant digits. Sensitivity analysis shows how sensitive the calculated answer is to percentage changes in the size of a particular component. It makes it possible to identify what are the most important parameters in terms of their influence on the final result. But it does not give any idea of the degree of accuracy of any particular number or of how the margin of error in any component affects the final answer.

For example, in cost – benefit analysis say, quantity of output (*Q*) in year *t* is estimated at 2410 units and price (*P*) at 19. The total value of output (*PQ* = *V*) is, then, 45,790. Sensitivity analysis would tell us that the answer is equally sensitive to quantity of output and to price, since

$$(Q \pm 0.1Q) P = (P \pm 0.1P)$$

That is, a 10 per cent change in either factor has the same effect on the result. Significant digits, however, would tell us that since the price (at 19) can be estimated only to two significant digits, the answer cannot have more than two significant digits. The value of output should, therefore, be given as 46,000 (rather than 45,790). Also, it is a waste of time to try to estimate the quantity of output more precisely than to the nearest hundred units. In this case, sensitivity analysis by itself could lead to a waste of effort: since the final answer here is as sensitive to the estimate of quantity of output as to price, it appears worthwhile to try to refine the number for quantity of output down to the tens and units place. Say a figure of 2413 units is finally estimated, giving an arithmetic total value of output of 45,847 (2413 × 19). In actual fact, the more accurate estimate would still be 46,000, the apparently greater precision of the 45,847 figure being spurious. If it were really important and possible to improve the time precision of the answer, then it would be necessary to estimate quantity to the hundreds or units place and price, at the same time, to the first or second decimal point.

Used correctly, sensitivity analysis can help the analyst or decision-maker to appreciate the range of uncertainty or imprecision involved in the numbers he is working with. For example, the range of variation in the final outcome can be charted showing the variation for all the inputs on a common abscissa as a percentage of the respective reported values and varying the estimates of the inputs, which are hardest to estimate within small limits, by e.g. ± 5 per cent, 10 per cent, 15 per cent, 20 per cent. This is more revealing than the associated technique of showing the results from making point estimates of the most likely values, of the pessimistic values — expected not to be exceeded in an unfavourable direction by more than, say, 5 per cent of the time — and of the optimistic values — expected to be bettered in outcome by no more than, say, 5 per cent of the time. Another useful technique to bring out the judgement of how great the uncertainty is, is to calculate how great a change in each of the different important elements of concern would be needed to reverse the final decision among the alternatives considered.

Very often the results of the usual type of sensitivity analysis are completely meaningless because they are swamped by the 'noise' in the numbers concerned. For example, the parameter being examined is taken as, say, '3167' when there is in reality one significant digit: the true number should have been written as 3000. A sensitivity analysis that tests a 10 per cent variation is in fact a useless exercise since the margin of error, ±500, in the number is greater than the ±317 of the variation tested.

Significant digits and probability analysis

The use of the technique of significant digits also has an impact on probability analysis. Probabilities change with how finely I try to slice reality: if I forecast the sales of widgets at 125,689 items for the current year, the probability of my being accurate is well below 0.001. If I estimate sales as 100,000 (implying a range, therefore, from 50,000 to 150,000) the probability I will prove right is many times higher.

The significant digit technique is much simpler to use and much easier to handle in computations. For many economic problems it is also more appropriate. Significant digit estimating allows one to bracket the area within which the true figure lies, it is much less demanding and it is often more honest than trying to estimate a set of probability distributions.

Bibliography

Adams, Arvil V. (1979) 'Who's in the Labor Force: A Simple Counting Problem?', *American Economic Review*, 69(2): 38 – 42.

Adams, Ernest W. (1965) 'Elements of a Theory of Inexact Measurement', *Philosophy of Science*, 32(3): 205 – 28.

Adelman, M. A. (1972) 'Review of Corporate control and business behavior', *Journal of Economic Literature*. 10(2) June: 493 – 5.

Allen, William R. (1974) 'Economics, Economists and Economic Policy: Modern American Experiences', paper presented to the Copenhagen Conferences of the Economic History Society.

American Agricultural Economic Association Committee on Economic Statistics (1972) 'Our Obsolete Data Systems: New Directions and Opportunities', *American Journal of Agricultural Economics*, 54(5): 867 – 75.

Arrow, Kenneth J. (1951) 'Mathematical Models in the Social Sciences', in Daniel Lerner and Harold D. Lasswell (eds), *The Policy Sciences*, Stanford, Calif.: Stanford University Press, pp. 129 – 54. Also printed as Cowles Commission Paper, New Series, 48.

—— (1957) 'Statistics and Economic Policy', *Econometrica*, 25(4): 523 – 31.

—— (1974a) 'Limited Knowledge and Economic Analysis', *American Economic Review*, 64(1): 1 – 10.

—— (1974b) 'The Measurement of Real Value Added', in Paul A. David and Melvin W. Reder (eds), *Nations and Households in Economic Growth: Essays in Honor of Moses Abramovitz*, New York and London: Academic Press, pp. 3 – 19.

Barco, Virgilio (1973) 'Statement in Discussion on Country Data Sheet', *Memorandum*, Washington, DC: World Bank, 4 Jan.

Bauer, P. T. and A. A. Walters (1975) 'The State of Economics', *Journal of Law and Economics* 18(1): 1 – 23.

Bauer, P. T. and B. S. Yarney (1957) *The Economics of Under-Developed Countries*. Cambridge: University Press.

Beckerman, Wilfred (1965) *International Comparisons of Real Incomes*,

Development Centre Studies no. 4 (Rev.), Paris: OECD Development Centre.

Bell, Carolyn Shaw (1977) 'Basic Data and Economic Policy', *Challenge*, 20(5): 43 – 9.

Bernhard, Richard C. (1960) 'Mathematics, Models, and Language in the Social Sciences', National Institute of Social and Behavioral Science, *Symposia Studies Series*, Washington, D.C.: George Washington Univ. No. 3: 1 – 5.

Black, Max (1970) *Margins of Precision. Essays in Logic and Language*, Ithaca and London: Cornell University Press.

Blaug, Mark (1980) *The Methodology of Economics*, Cambridge, etc.: Cambridge University Press.

Bonnen, James T. (1975) 'Improving Information on Agriculture and Rural Life', Presidential Address, Proceedings Issue, *American Journal of Agricultural Economics*, 57(5): 753 – 63.

Board of Governors of Federal Reserve System (1983) *Bulletin*, 69(2) February: A45, A53.

Borders, William (1979) 'Taxing Britain's Company Car', *New York Times* 128 (44322) Aug. 27: D1,4.

Boulding, Kenneth (1970) *Economics as a Science*, New York, St. Louis, etc.: McGraw-Hill.

Brunner, Karl (1973) Review of *Econometric Models of Cyclical Behavior*, *American Economic Review*, 11(3): 926 – 33.

Bruton, Henry J. (1978) 'Unemployment Problems and Policies in Less Developed Countries', *American Economic Review*, 68(2): 51 – 5.

Cairncross, Alec [1976] 'The Limitations of Shadow Rates', in Alec Cairncross and Mohinder Puri (eds), *Employment, Income Distribution and Development Strategy: Problems of the Developing Countries*, Essays in Honor of H. W. Singer, New York: Holmes & Meier, pp. 169 – 80.

—— (1969) 'Economic Forecasting', Presidential Address to the Royal Economic Society, 3 July 1969, *Economic Journal*, 79(316): 797 – 812.

Caws, Peter (1959) 'Definition and Measurement in Physics', in C. West Churchman and Pilburn Ratoosh (eds), *Measurement, Definitions and Theories*, New York and London: John Wiley, pp. 3 – 17.

CERES (1978) 'Measuring Human Progress', Rome: FAO: 10 – 12.

Chandler, Alfred D., Jr (1977) *The Visible Hand: The Managerial Revolution in American Business*, Cambridge, Mass. and London, England: Harvard University Press.

Chenery, Hollis B. and Lance Taylor (1968) 'Development Patterns: among Countries and over Time', *The Review of Economics and Statistics*, 50: 391 – 416.

Chenery, Hollis B. *et al.* (1974) *Redistribution with Growth*, London: Oxford University Press.

Christ, Carl F. (1952) 'History of the Cowles Commission, 1932 – 1952', *Economic Theory and Measurement. A Twenty Year Research Report*

1932 – 1952, Cowles Commission for Research in Economics, University of Chicago. Baltimore: The Waverly Press, pp. 3 – 65.

—— [1966] *Econometric Models and Methods*, New York, London and Sydney: John Wiley.

Churchman, C. West (1948) *Theory of Experimental Inference*, New York: Macmillan.

Clague, Christopher (1977) 'Information Costs, Corporate Hierarchies, and Earnings Inequality', *American Economic Review*, 67(1) Feb.: 81 – 5.

Crousse, Bernard (1972) 'Esquisse de quelques éléments d'une problématique et d'une méthodologie de la science économique', *Technique économique et finalité humaine*, Namur: CERUNA, Editions Duculot Gembloux, pp. 219 – 59.

Cyert, Richard M. and Charles L. Hedrick (1972) 'Theory of the Firm: Past, Present and Future; An Interpretation', *Journal of Economic Literature*, 10(2): 398 – 409.

Dasgupta, A. K. (1968) *Methodology of Economic Research,* Bombay, etc.: Asia Publishing House.

Davidson, Paul (1981) 'Post Keynesian Economics', in Daniel Bell and Irving Kristol (eds), *The Crisis in Economic Theory*, New York: Basic Books, pp. 151 – 73.

De V. Graaff, J. (1975) 'Cost – Benefit Analysis: A Critical View', *The South African Journal of Economics*, 43(2): 233-44.

Denison, Edward F. (1973) 'The Shift to Services and the Rate of Productivity Change' Technical Series Reprint T-003 from *Survey of Current Business*, 53(10), Washington, DC: Brookings Institution, pp. 20 – 35.

Devons, Ely [1961] *Essays in Economics*, London: George Allen & Unwin.

DeWulf, Luc (1978) 'Fiscal Aspects of Customs Valuation and the Faking of Invoices', *International Monetary Fund Departmental Memoranda*, DM 78/60, Fiscal Affairs Department, 27 June, pp. 1 – 31.

Dorfman, Robert (1972) 'Economics of Pollution — Discussion', *American Economic Review*, 63(2): 253 – 6.

—— (1977) 'Incidence of the Benefits and Costs of Environmental Programs', *American Economic Review*, 67(1): 333 – 40.

Drucker, Peter F. (1978) 'Meaningful Unemployment Figures', *Wall Street Journal*, 192(88), Eastern edition, 3 Nov., p. 20.

—— (1979) *Adventures of a Bystander*, New York etc.: Harper & Row.

Dunlop, John T. (1977) 'Industrial Relations, Labor Economics, and Policy Decisions', Presidential Address to the Fourth World Congress of the International Industrial Relations Association, Geneva, Sept. 1976. Reprinted in *Challenge*, 20(3): 6 – 12.

Dunn, Edgar S. (1974) *Social Information Processing and Statistical Systems — Change and Reform*, New York, London, etc.: John Wiley.

Easterlin, R. A. (1974) 'Does Economic Growth Improve the Human

Lot? Some Empirical Evidence', in Paul A. David and Melvin W. Reder (eds), *Nations and Households in Economic Growth: Essays in Honor of Moses Abramovitz*, New York and London: Academic Press, pp. 89 – 125.

Eckstein, Otto (1978) 'How Have Forecasts Worked? Discussion', *American Economic Review*, 68(2): 320 – 1.

Economist, The (1977) 'Population: Take three guesses and rule none out', 264(6979), 4 June: 25.

—— (1980a) 'Digging into the black hole', 274(7123) 8 Mar.:72.

—— (1980b) 'Hungary. The Quiet Revolution', 276(7151), 20 Sept.: 68 – 71.

—— (1980c) 'India's private sector: red tape, black money, white hope', 277(7154), 11 Oct.: 79.

—— (1981) 'How many beans make five?' 280(7201) 14 Nov.:103.

Fabricant, Solomon (1972) 'Productivity in the Tertiary Sector', *National Bureau Report Supplement*, No. 10, New York: National Bureau of Economic Research, pp. 1 – 10.

Feldman, Jerome A. (1979) 'Programming Languages', *Scientific American*, 241(6): 94 – 116.

Feldstein, Martin (1978) 'The Effect of Unemployment Insurance on Temporary Layoff Unemployment', *American Economic Review*, 68(5): 834 – 46.

Finegan, T. Aldrich (1978) 'Should Discouraged Workers be Counted as Unemployed?' *Challenge*, 21(5): 20 – 5.

Fisher, Irving (1927), *The Nature of Capital and Income*, New York: Macmillan.

Foldesay, Edward P. and Gene G. Marcial (1979) 'Fed's Mistake on Money Supply Raises Questions on Data-Reporting Safeguards', *Wall Street Journal*, 194(84), Eastern edition, 29 Oct., p. 2.

Forbes (1980) 'The way it wasn't' 125(8), 14 April:144.

Friedman, Milton (1953) 'The Methodology of Positive Economics', *Essays in Positive Economics*, Chicago: University of Chicago Press.

Garcia, Gillian and Simon Pak (1979) 'Some Clues in the Case of the Missing Money', *American Economic Review*, 69(2): 330 – 4.

Garside, W. R. (1980) *The Measurement of Unemployment*, Oxford: Basil Blackwell.

Geertz, Clifford (1978) 'The Bazaar Economy: Information and Search in Peasant Marketing', *American Economic Review*, 68(2): 28 – 32.

Georgescu-Roegen, Nicholas (1958) 'The Nature of Expectation and Uncertainty', in Mary Jean Bowman (ed.), *Expectations, Uncertainty and Business Behavior*. A conference held at Carnegie Institute of Technology, 27 – 29 October 1955, under the auspices of the Committee on Business Enterprise Research. Part K, No. I, New York: Social Science Research Council, pp. 11 – 29.

—— (1967) *Analytical Economics Issues and Problems*, Cambridge, Mass.: Harvard University Press.

—— (1971) *The Entropy Law and the Economic Process*, Cambridge,

Mass.: Harvard University Press.

—— (1976) 'Economic Growth and its Representation by Models', *Atlantic Economic Journal*, 4(1): 1 – 8.

Ginzberg, Eli (1977) 'The Job Problem', *Scientific American*, 237(5): 43 – 51.

Greene, Richard (1982) 'Men of goodwill, disagreeing', *Forbes*, 130(12), 6 Dec.: 168, 171.

Griliches, Zvi (1963) 'Capital Stock in Investment Functions: Some Problems of Concept and Measurement', *Measurement in Economics*, Studies in Mathematical Economics and Econometrics in Memory of Yehuda Grunfeld, by Carl F. Christ, and others, Stanford, Calif.: Stanford University Press, pp. 115 – 37.

Guisinger, Stephen and Demetrios Papageorgiou (1976) 'The Selection of apppropriate Border Prices in Project Evaluation', *Oxford Bulletin of Economics and Statistics*, 38(2): 79 – 98.

Hahn, F. H. (1970) 'Some Adjustment Problems', Presidential Address, Dec. 1968, Econometric Society, *Econometrica*, 38(1): 1 – 17.

—— (1981) 'General Equilibrium Theory' in Daniel Bell and Irving Kristol (eds), *The Crisis in Economic Theory*, New York: Basic Books, pp. 123 – 38.

Hall, R. E. (1978) 'The Nature and Measurement of Unemployment', *NBER Working Paper*, No. 252.

—— (1979) 'Letter', *Fortune*, 100(6), 24 Sept.: 144.

Haq, Mahbub ul (1976) *The Poverty Curtain: Choices for the Third World*, New York: Columbia University Press.

Harberger, Arnold (1972) 'On Measuring the Social Opportunity Cost of Labor', in ILO, *Fiscal Measures for Employment Generation in Developing Countries*, Geneva: International Labor Office, pp. 3 – 24.

Harcourt, G. C. (1971) 'Review of Michio Morishima, *Theory of Economic Growth*', *Journal of Economic Literature*, 9(1): 91 – 2.

Harris, Ralph (1977) 'Models or Markets? A Skeptical View of Forecasting in Britain', in James B. Ramsey, *Economic Forecasting — Models or Markets*? Hobart Paper 74, London: Institute of Economic Affairs, pp. 81 – 101.

Haveman, Robert H. (1978) 'Unemployment in Western Europe and the United States: A Problem of Demand, Structure, or Measurement?' *American Economic Review*, 68(2): 44 – 50.

Hayek, F. A. (1975) 'The Pretence of Knowledge', (Nobel Memorial Prize Lecture), in *Full Employment at any Price*? London: Institute of Economic Affairs, pp. 30 – 42.

Helleiner, Gerald K. (1981) *Intra-Firm Trade and the Developing Countries*, New York: St. Martin's Press.

Hendry, David. F. (1980) 'Econometrics — Alchemy or Science?' *Economica*, 47: 387 – 406.

Herman, Edward S. (1981) *Corporate Control, Corporate Power*, Cambridge, etc.: Cambridge University Press.

146   *Bibliography*

Hicks, John (1977) *Economic Perspectives: Further Essays on Money and Growth*, Oxford: Clarendon Press.
—— (1979) *Causality in Economics*, New York: Basic Books.
—— (1981) *Wealth and Welfare*, Collected Essays on Economic Theory, Vol. I, Cambridge, Mass.: Harvard University Press; Oxford: Basil Blackwell.
Hill, T. P. (1971) *The Measurement of Real Product*, Paris: Organisation for Economic Co-operation and Development.
Hirsch, Fred (1976) *Social Limits to Growth*, Twentieth Century Fund Study, Cambridge, Mass: Harvard University Press.
Hofstadter, Douglas R. (1979) *Goedel, Escher, Bach: an Eternal Golden Braid*, New York: Basic Books.
Holland, Edward P. (1970) 'Simulating the Dynamics of Economic Development', *Economics Dept. Working Paper*, No. 90, World Bank, mimeo., 28 Oct.
Hutchison, T. W. (1977) *Knowledge and Ignorance in Economics*, Oxford: Basil Blackwell.
International Monetary Fund (1977) *Balance of Payments Manual*, 4th edn, Washington, DC: International Monetary Fund.
Johnson, H. G. (1964) 'Comments on Mr John Vaizey's Paper', *The Residual Factor and Economic Growth*, Paris: Organization for Economic Co-operation and Development, pp. 219 – 27.
—— (1977) 'Methodologies of Economics', in Mark Perlman (ed.), *The Organization and Retrieval of Economic Knowledge*, Proceedings, Conference of International Economic Association, Kiel, West Germany. Boulder, Colo.: Westview Press, pp. 496 – 509.
Juster, F. Thomas (1973) 'A Framework for the Measurement of Economic and Social Performance', in Milton Moss (ed.), *The Measurement of Economic and Social Performance*, New York: National Bureau of Economic Research.
——, Paul N. Courant and Greg Dow (1981) 'A Theoretical Framework for the Measurement of Well-Being', *Review of Income and Wealth*, 27(1): 1 – 31.
Kaldor, Nicholas (1972) 'The Irrelevance of Equilibrium Economies', *Economic Journal*, 82(328): 1237 – 55.
Kamarck, Andrew M. (1965) 'Notes on Underemployment', in E. F. Jackson (ed.), *Economic Development in Africa: Papers Presented to the Nyasaland Economic Symposium held in Blantyre 18 to 28 July 1962*, Oxford: Basil Blackwell, pp. 78 – 85.
—— (1976) *The Tropics and Economic Development*, The World Bank, Baltimore and London: The Johns Hopkins Press.
Katona, George (1975) *Psychological Economics*, New York, Oxford, Amsterdam: Elsevier.
Katsenelinboigen, Aron (1978 – 79) 'L. V. Kantorovich: The political dilemma in scientific creativity', *Journal of Post Keynesian Economics*, 1(2) Winter: 129 – 47.
Katz, Daniel (1972) 'Psychology in Economic Affairs', in Burkhard

Strumpel *et al*, (eds), *Human Behavior in Economic Affairs*, Amsterdam, etc.: Elsevier, pp. 57 – 81.

Keynes, John Maynard (1925) 'Alfred Marshall, 1842 – 1924', in A. C. Pigou (ed.), *Memorials of Alfred Marshall*, London: Macmillan, pp. 1 – 65.

—— [1936] *The General Theory of Employment, Interest and Money*, New York: Harcourt Bros.

—— (1962) *A Treatise on Probability*, New York and Evanston: Harper & Row.

Kilmister, C. W. (1977) 'Mathematics in the Social Sciences', in Ronald Duncan and Miranda Weston-Smith (eds), *The Encyclopedia of Ignorance*, Oxford, New York, etc.: Pergamon Press, reprinted 1978, pp. 175 – 89.

King, Benjamin B. (1968) 'Notes on the Mechanics of Growth and Debt', *World Bank Occasional Papers*, Baltimore, Md.: The Johns Hopkins Press.

—— (1981) 'What is a SAM? A Layman's Guide to Social Accounting Matrices', *World Bank Staff Working Papers*, No. 463, Washington, DC: The World Bank.

Klein, Frederick C. (1978) 'Underground Inc.' Wall Street Journal Eastern edition, 192(106) 30 Nov.: 1,29.

Knight, Frank Hyneman (1924) 'The Limitations of Scientific Method in Economics', in Rexford Guy Tugwell (ed.), *The Trend of Economics*, New York: Alfred A. Knopf, pp. 227 – 67.

—— (1956) '"What is Truth" in Economics?' on *On the History and Method of Economics*, Chicago: University of Chicago Press, pp. 151 – 78.

—— (1971) *Risk, Uncertainty and Profit*, Chicago and London: University of Chicago Press.

Koerner, Stephan (1966) *Experience and Theory. An Essay in the Philosophy of Science*, London: Routledge and Kegan Paul.

Koopmans, Tjalling C. (1957) *Three Essays on the State of Economic Science*, New York, Toronto, London: McGraw Hill.

—— (1970) 'Measurement without Theory', 'Methodological Issues in Quantitative Economics — A Reply', 'Statistical Estimation of Simultaneous Economic Relations', in *Scientific Papers of Tjalling C. Koopmans*, Berlin, Heidelberg, New York: Springer-Verlag, 112 – 31, 148 – 56, 92 – 111.

Kornai, Janos (1971) *Anti-Equilibrium: On Economic Systems Theory and the Tasks of Research*, Amsterdam: North Holland.

Koten, John and Amanda Bennett (1981) 'Sticker Stickler. Auto Makers Rethink Pricing Policies . . .', *Wall Street Journal*, 198(81) Eastern edition, 23 Oct., p. 1.

Kravis, Irving B. *et al.* (1975) *A System of International Comparisons of Gross Product and Purchasing Power*, United Nations International Comparison Project: Phase one, Baltimore and London: Johns Hopkins Press for World Bank.

Kravis, Irving B. and Robert E. Lipsey (1977) 'Export Prices and the Transmission of Inflation', *American Economic Review*, 67(19): 155 – 63.

Kristol, Irving (1981) 'Rationalism in Economics', in Daniel Bell and Irving Kristol, (eds), *The Crisis in Economic Theory*, New York: Basic Books, pp. 201 – 18.

Kunreuther, Howard and Paul Slovic (1978) 'Economics, Psychology, and Protective Behavior', *American Economic Review*, 68(2): 64 – 9.

Kuznets, Simon [1965, 1968] *Toward a Theory of Economic Growth*, New York: W. W. Norton.

—— (1966) *Modern Economic Growth*, New Haven and London: Yale University Press.

—— (1973) 'Concluding Remarks' in Milton Moss (ed.), *The Measurement of Economic and Social Performance*, New York: National Bureau of Economic Research, pp. 589 – 92.

Lanzillotti, Robert F. (1958) 'Pricing Objectives in Large Companies', *American Economic Review*, 48(5): 921 – 40.

Lawson, Tony (1981) 'Keynesian Model Building and the Rational Expectations Critique', *Cambridge Journal of Economics*, 5: 311 – 26.

Leff, Laurel (1978) 'Trading Flourishes on Many Exchanges You Never Heard of', *Wall Street Journal*, 192(48), Eastern edition, 8 Sept.: 1, 19.

Leibenstein, Harvey (1976) *Beyond Economic Man*, Cambridge, Mass. and London, England: Harvard University Press.

—— (1977) 'X-Efficiency, Technical Efficiency, and Incomplete Information Use: A Comment', *Economic Development and Cultural Change*, 25(2): 311 – 16.

—— (1978a) 'X-Inefficiency Xists — Reply to an Xorcist', *American Economic Review*, 68(1): 203 – 11.

—— (1978b) 'On the Basic Proposition of X-Efficiency Theory', *American Economic Review*, 68(2): 328 – 32.

—— (1979) 'A Branch of Economics is Missing: Micro-Micro Theory', *Journal of Economic Literature*, 17(2): 477 – 502.

Leontief, Wassily (1971) 'Theoretical Assumptions and Nonobserved Facts', presidential address to American Economic Association, 29 Dec. 1970, *American Economic Review*, 61(1): 1 – 7.

—— (1982) 'Academic Economics', *Science*, 217(4555), 9 July: 104, 107.

Liber, Paul (1962) 'Report on First Mission to the Israel Institute of Technology in Haifa as UNESCO Expert in Engineering Science' 25 Nov. 1960 to 5 Jan. 1961, mimeo, 27 March, pp. 40.

Lindblom, Charles E. (1959) 'The Science of "Muddling Through"', *Public Administration Review*, 19(2): 79 – 88.

Little, I. M .D. (1957) *A Critique of Welfare Economics*, 2nd edn, Oxford: Clarendon Press.

Little, I. M. D. and Mirrlees, J. A. (1968) *Manual of Industrial Project Analysis in Developing Countries, Vol. II, Social Cost – Benefit Analysis*, Paris: OECD Development Centre.

—— (1974) *Project Appraisal and Planning for Developing Countries*,

London: Heinemann Educational Books.

Loeb, Martin and Wesley A. Magat (1978) 'Success Indicators in the Soviet Union: The Problem of Incentives and Efficient Allocation', *American Economic Review*, 68(1): 173 – 81.

Lowe, Adolph (1965) *On Economic Knowledge*, World Perspectives: vol. 35, ed. by Ruth Nanda Ashen, New York and Evanston: Harper & Row.

Maisel, Sherman J. (1972) 'Reflections on Monetary Policy', *Washington Post*, 23 April: F1.

—— (1973) *Managing the Dollar*, New York: W. W. Norton Co.

—— (1974) 'The Economic and Financial Literature and Decision Making', *Journal of Finance*, 29: 313 – 22.

Margenau, Henry (1959) 'Philosophical Problems Concerning the Meaning of Measurement in Physics', in C. West Churchman and Philburn Ratoosh, *Measurement: Definitions and Theories*, New York and London: John Cutley & Sons, pp. 163 – 76.

Marris, Robin and Dennis C. Mueller (1980) 'The Corporation, Competition and the Invisible Hand', *Journal of Economic Literature*, 18(1): 32 – 63.

Marshall, Alfred (1925) 'Letter to Bowley', in A. C. Pigou (ed.), *Memorials of Alfred Marshall*, London: Macmillan, 3.iii.01, pp. 421 – 3; 7.x.06, pp. 428 – 9.

—— (1952) *Principles of Economics*, 8th edn, London: Macmillan.

Mason, Edward S. (1958) *Economic Planning in Underdeveloped Areas: Government and Business*, New York: Fordham University Press.

—— (ed.) (1959) *The Corporation in Modern Society*, Cambridge, Mass.: Harvard University Press. Seventh printing 1970.

Mayer, Thomas (1980) 'Economics as a Hard Science: Realistic Goal or Wishful Thinking?' *Economic Inquiry*, 28: 165 – 78.

Menger, Karl (1967) 'The Role of Uncertainty in Economics', in Martin Shubik (ed.), *Essays in Mathematical Economics*, Princeton, NJ: Princeton University Press, pp. 211 – 31.

McKenzie, Richard B. (1978) 'On the Methodological Boundaries of Economic Analysis', *Journal of Economics Issues*, 12(2): 627 – 45.

McKinley, John K. (1982) 'A Time of Change', *The Texaco Star*, 69(2): 1 – 3.

McNees, Stephen K. (1978) 'How Have Forecasts Worked? The "Rationality" of Economic Forecasts', *American Economic Review*, 68(2): 301 – 5.

Michael, Walther P. (1971) *Measuring International Capital Movements*, Occasional Paper 114, New York: National Bureau of Economic Research.

Miller, George (1956) 'The Magical Number Seven, Plus or Minus Two', *Psychological Review*, 63.

Mills, Frederick Cecil (1924) 'On Measurement in Economics', in Rexford Guy Tugwell (ed.), *The Trend of Economics*, New York: Alfred A. Knopf, pp. 37 – 72.

Mishan, E. J. (1967) 'A Survey of Welfare Economics, 1939 – 59', *Surveys of Economic Theory, Money, Interest, and Welfare*, prepared for the American Economic Association and the Royal Economic Society, Vol. I, New York: St Martin's Press; London, etc.: Macmillan, pp. 154 – 222.

—— (1971) *Cost – Benefit Analysis: An Introduction*, New York, Washington: Praeger.

Modigliani, Franco and Kalman J. Cohen (1955) 'The Significance and Uses of Ex Ante Data', in Mary Jean Bowman (ed.), *Expectations, Uncertainty and Business Behavior*, a conference, Carnegie Institute of Technology, 27 – 29 October, 1955, New York: Social Science Research Council, pp. 151 – 64.

Moore, Geoffrey H. (1977) 'A Continuing Audit of Government Economic Statistics', *Challenge*: 29 – 33.

Morgan, James H. (1978) 'Multiple Motives, Group Decisions, Uncertainty, Ignorance, and Confusion: A Realistic Economics of the Consumer Requires Some Psychology', *American Economic Review*, 68(2): 58 – 63.

Morgan, Theodore (1969) 'Investment versus Economic Growth', *Economic Development and Cultural Change*, 17(3): 392 – 414.

Morgenstern, Oskar (1974) 'Letter, February 11, 1974'. Reproduced in *Forum for Contemporary History*, Skeptic, Part 2, pp. 1 – 4.

—— (1937) *The Limits of Economics*, tr. by Vera Smith, London, etc.: William Hodge.

—— (1963) *On the Accuracy of Economic Observations*, 2nd edn, Princeton, NJ: Princeton University Press.

Morris, Frank E. (1980) 'Do the Monetary Aggregates Have a Future as Targets of Federal Reserve Policy?' *New England Economic Review*, 5 – 23.

Moss, Milton (1973a) 'Introduction', in Milton Moss (ed.), *The Measurement of Economic and Social Performance*, New York: National Bureau of Economic Research.

—— (ed.) (1973b) *The Measurement of Economic and Social Performance*, No. 38 by the Conference on Research in Income and Wealth, New York: National Bureau of Economic Research.

Myrdal, Gunnar (1968) *Asian Drama: An Inquiry into the Poverty of Nations*, New York: Random House – Pantheon.

Nagel, Ernest (1963) 'Assumptions in Economic Theory', *American Economic Review*, 53(2): 211 – 19.

National Bureau of Economic Research (1972) *National Bureau Report*, 10, New York: NBER, pp. 1 – 21.

Naya, Seiji and Theodore Morgan (1974) 'The Accuracy of International Trade Data: The Case of Southeast Asian Countries', in Jagdish N. Bhagwati, *Illegal Transactions in International Trade*, Amsterdam, Oxford, New York: American Elsevier, pp. 123 – 37.

Nelson, Richard A. and Sidney G. Winter (1977) 'Simulation of Schumpeterian Competition', *American Economic Review*, 67(1): 271 – 6.

New York Times (1978) 'Stronger Marijuana Sold Here Stirs Fresh Debate', 28 Dec., Metropolitan Report, NY, NJ, Conn, pp. B1, B6.

Orcutt, Guy (1970) 'Data Research and Government', *American Economic Review*, 60(2): 133 – 4.

Organization for Economic Co-operation and Development (1982a) 'The Hidden Economy', *Occasional Studies, OECD Economic Outlook*, Paris, pp. 28 – 45.

—— (1982b) 'The World Current Account Discrepancy', *Occasional Studies, OECD Economic Outlook*, Paris, pp. 46 – 63.

Park, Thae S. (1981) 'Relationship between Personal Income and Adjusted Gross Income, 1947 – 78', US Dept. of Commerce, *Survey of Current Business*, 61(11): 24 – 8, 41.

Patinkin, Don (1976) 'Keynes and Econometrics: On the Interaction between the Macroeconomic Revolutions of the Interwar Period', *Econometrica*, 44(6): 1091 – 123.

Penner, Rudy G. (1978) 'The Mid-Year Budget Outlook', *NEC Abstracts*, Ruth Logue, Rapporteur, The National Economists Club, Washington, DC address given 18 July, 1978, mimeo, 2 p.

Perlman, Mark (1978) 'Review of *Knowledge and Ignorance in Economics* by T. W. Hutchison', *Journal of Economic Literature*, 16(2): 582 – 5.

Pfanzagl, J. (1968) *Theory of Measurement*, Würzburg – Wien: Physica-Verlag.

Phelps Brown, E. H. (1972) 'The Underdevelopment of Economics', Presidential Address to the Royal Economic Society, 8 July 1971, *The Economic Journal*, 82(325): 1 – 10.

Pigou, A. C. (ed.) (1925) *Memorials of Alfred Marshall*, London: Macmillan.

—— (1935) 'An Economist's *Apologia*', in *Economics in Practice*, London: Macmillan.

Popper, Karl (1964) *Conjectures and Reputations*, London: Gollancz.

Reich-Ranicki, Marcel (1980) 'Open Questions before Chinese Walls', *Encounter*, 55(4): 62 – 8.

Review of Economics and Statistics (1954) 'Mathematics in Economics', articles by David Novick, Paul A. Samuelson, L. R. Klein, James S. Duesenberry, John S. Chipman, J. Tinbergen, D. G. Champerowne, Robert Solow, Robert Dorfman, Tjalling C. Koopmans, 36(4): 357 – 86.

Reynolds, Lloyd G. (1971) *The Three Worlds of Economics*, New Haven, Conn. and London: Yale University Press.

—— (1977) *Image and Reality in Economic Development*, New Haven, Conn. and London: Yale University Press.

Roberts, Marc J. (1974) 'On the Nature and Condition of Social Science', *Daedalus*. Issued as 103(3), *Proceedings of American Academy of Arts & Sciences*, pp. 47 – 64.

Robbins, Lionel (1962) *An Essay on the Nature and Significance of Economic Science*, 2nd edn, rev. and extended, London: Macmillan; New York: St Martin's Press.

Robinson, Joan (1965) *The Accumulation of Capital*, London: Macmillan.
—— (1977) 'What are the Questions?' *Journal of Economic Literature*, 15(4): 1318 – 39.
Routh, Guy (1967) 'The Evolution of an Economist', *Monthly Labor Review*: 18 – 22.
—— (1977) 'The Mist in Economics', *New York Times*, 8 Nov. p. 33.
Rubner, Alex [1970] (1971) *Three Sacred Cows of Economics*, New York: Barnes and Noble.
Rudd, Ernest (1954 – 55) 'The Accuracy of Data Collected from Firms', *Journal of Industrial Economics*, 3: 72 – 7.
Rudra, Ashok (1969) *Measurement in Economics*, G. N. Sinha Institute of Social Studies, Monograph 1, Bombay, Calcutta, New Delhi, etc: Allied Publishers.
Ruggles, Nancy D. (1964) 'Review of *On the Accuracy of Economic Observations . . .* by Oskar Morgenstern . . .', *American Economic Review*, 54(4): 445 – 7.
Ruggles, Richard (1959) 'The U.S. National Accounts and their Development', A Review Article, *American Economic Review*, 43(1): 85 – 95.
Salamon, Gerald L. and E. Dan Smith (1979) 'Corporate control and managerial misrepresentation of firm performance', *Bell Journal of Economics*, 10(1) Spring: 319 – 28.
Samuels, Warren J. (1978) 'Normative Premises in Regulatory Theory', *Journal of Post Keynesian Economics*, 1(1): 100 – 14.
Samuelson, Paul A. (1962) 'Economists and the History of Ideas', Presidential Address delivered at the annual meeting of the American Economic Association, New York, 27 Dec. 1961, *American Economic Review*, 52(1): 1 – 18.
—— (1963) 'Problems of Methodology — Discussion', *American Economic Review*, 53(2): 231 – 6.
—— (1964) 'A Brief Post-Keynesian Survey', in R. Lekachman (ed.), *Keynes's General Theory, Reports of Three Decades*, New York: St Martin's Press; London: Macmillan, pp. 331 – 47. Quoted in T. W. Hutchison, 1977, pp. 147 – 8.
Schmedtje, Jochen K. (1965) 'On Estimating the Economic Cost of Capital', *IBRD Report*, No. EC-138, Washington, DC: International Bank for Reconstruction & Development, 21 October, mimeo.
Schoeffler, Sidney (1955) *The Failures of Economics: A Diagnostic Study*, Cambridge, Mass.: Harvard University Press.
Schultz, George P. (1974) 'Reflections on Political Economy', *Journal of Finance*, 29(2): 323 – 30.
Schumpeter, Joseph A. (1949) *The Theory of Economic Development*, Cambridge, Mass.: Harvard University Press.
Scitovsky, Tibor (1976) *The Joyless Economy: An Inquiry into Human Satisfaction and Consumer Dissatisfaction*, Oxford, London, New York: Oxford University Press.
Schwartz, Hugh and Richard Barney (eds) (1977) *Social and Economic*

Dimensions of Project Evaluation, Symposium on 'The Use of Socioeconomic Investment Criteria in Project Evaluation', Washington, DC: Inter-American Bank.

Seers, Dudley [1967] 'The Limitations of the Special Case', in Kurt Martin and John Knapp (eds), *The Teaching of Development Economics*, Chicago: Aldine, pp. 1 – 27.

—— [1976] 'The Political Economy of National Accounting', in Alec Cairncross and Mohinder Puri (eds), *Employment, Income Distribution and Development Strategy: Problems of the Developing Countries*, Essays in Honor of H. W. Singer, New York: Holmes & Meier, pp. 193 – 209.

Sen, Amartya (1979) 'Personal Utilities and Public Judgments: or What's Wrong with Welfare Economics?' *Economic Journal*, 89:537 – 58.

Serrin, William (1981) 'No Cuts Here: The Life on the Tab', *New York Times*, 130 (44902), 29 Mar. Sect. 3, pp. 1, 15.

Shackle, G. L. S. (1955) *Uncertainty in Economics and Other Reflections*, Cambridge: Cambridge University Press. Reprinted 1968.

Shourie, Arun (1972) 'The Use of Macro-economic Regression Models of Developing Countries for Forecasts and Policy Prescription', *Oxford Economic Papers*, 24(1): 1-35.

Simon, Herbert A. (1954) 'Some Strategic Considerations in the Construction of Social Science Models', in Paul F. Lazarfeld, *Mathematical Thinking in the Social Sciences*, New York: Russell & Russell, pp. 385 – 415. Reissued 1969.

—— (1963) 'Problems of Methodology — Discussion', *American Economic Review*, 53(2): 229 – 31.

—— (1978) 'On How to Decide What to Do', *The Bell Journal of Economics*, 9(2): 494 – 507.

—— (1979) 'Rational Decision Making in Business Organizations', *American Economic Review*, 69(4): 493 – 513.

Smith, John S. (1966) 'Asymmetries and Errors in Reported Balance of Payments Statistics', International Monetary Fund, DM/66/67, 5 Dec., mimeo, pp. 1 – 25.

Smith, Vernon L. (1970) 'Investment Behavior — Discussion', *American Economic Review*, 40(2).

Smyth, D. J. and J. C. K. Ash (1975) 'Notes and Memoranda: Forecasting Gross National Product, the Rate of Inflation and the Balance of Trade: the OECD Performance', *The Economic Journal*, 85(338): 361 – 4.

Solo, Robert A. (1974) 'Review Article: Arithomorphism and Entropy', *Economic Development and Cultural Change*, 22(3): 510 – 17.

Squire, Lynn and Herman G. van der Tak (1975) *Economic Analysis of Projects*, Baltimore, Ind.: Johns Hopkins Press for World Bank.

Stewart, Frances (1978) 'Book Review of *Project Appraisal in Practice* by M. F. G. Scott, J. D. MacArthur and D. M. Newbery', *Journal of Development Studies*, 14(2): 254 – 6.

—— and Paul Streeten (1972) 'Little – Mirrlees Methods and Project

Appraisal', *Bulletin*, Oxford University Institute of Economics and Statistics, 34(1): 75 – 91.

Stigler, George (1959) 'The Politics of Political Economists', *Quarterly Journal of Economics*, 73(4): 529 – 30.

—— (1961) 'The Economics of Information', *Journal of Political Economy*, 62: 213 – 25.

—— (1976) 'The Xistence of X-Efficiency', *American Economic Review*, 66(1): 213 – 16.

Stiglitz, Joseph E. and Michael J. Boskin (1977) 'Some Lessons from the New Public Finance', *American Economic Review*, 67(1): 295 – 301.

Stolper, Wolfgang F. (1966) *Planning Without Facts*, Cambridge, Mass.: Harvard University Press.

—— (1969) *Limitations of Comprehensive Planning in the Face of Comprehensive Uncertainty: Crisis of Planning or Crisis of Planners*, Discussion Paper No. 10, Ann Arbor, Mich.: Center for Research on Economic Development, University of Michigan, 44 pp.

Stone, Christopher (1976) *Where the Law Ends: The Social Control of Corporate Behavior*, New York etc.: Harper & Row.

Stone, Lawrence (1979) 'In the Alleys of Mentalite', *New York Review of Books*, 26(17), 8 Nov.: 20 – 4.

Stone, Richard and S. J. Prais (1952) 'Systems of Aggregate Index Numbers and their Compatibility', *Economic Journal*, 62(247): 565 – 83.

Stouffer, Samuel A. *et al.* (1950) *Measurement and Prediction*, Studies in Social Psychology in World War II, vol. IV, Princeton, NJ: Princeton University Press.

Stout, Russell, Jr (1980) *Management or Control? The Organizational Challenge*, Bloomington and London: Indiana University Press.

Streeten, Paul (1972) *The Frontiers of Development Studies*, New York: John Wiley & Sons.

—— (1973) 'The Multinational Enterprise and the Theory of Develop ment Policy', *World Development*, 1(10): 1 – 14.

Strumpel, Burkhard *et al.* (eds) (1972) *Human Behaviour in Economic Affairs, Essays in Honor of George Katona*, Amsterdam, London, New York: Elsevier.

Su, Vincent (1978) 'How Have Forecasts Worked? An Error Analysis of Econometric and Noneconometric Forecasts', *American Economic Review*, 68(2): 306 – 12.

Sullivan, Walter (1979) 'A Vast "Interdisciplinary Effort" to Predict Climate Trend Urged', *New York Times*, 24 Feb., p. 44.

Thurow, Lester C. (1977) 'Economics 1977', *Daedalus*, Journal of American Academy of Arts & Sciences, 2: 79 – 94.

Tinbergen, Jan and H. C. Bos (1962) *Mathematical Models of Economic Growth*, New York: McGraw-Hill.

Tintner, Gerhard (1966) 'Some Thoughts about the State of Econometrics', in Sherman Roy Krupp (ed.), *The Structure of Economic Science*, Englewood Cliffs, NJ: Prentice-Hall, pp. 114 – 28.

Titmuss, Richard M. (1962) *Income Distribution and Social Change: A Study in Criticism*, London: George Allen & Unwin.

Todaro, Michael (1969) 'A Model of Labor Migration and Urban Unemployment in Less Developed Countries', *American Economic Review*, 59(1): 138 – 88.

Triplett, Jack E. (1975) 'The Measurement of Inflation: A Survey of Research on the Accuracy of Price Indexes', in Paul H. Earl, (ed.), *Analysis of Inflation*, Lexington, Mass.: Lexington Books, D. C. Heath, pp. 19 – 82.

—— (1977) 'Measuring Prices and Wages', *American Economic Review*, 67(1): 135 – 40.

United Nations (1968) *A System of National Accounts*, Statistical Office, Studies in Methods, New York: United Nations.

UNIDO (1972) *Guidelines for Project Evaluation*, by P. S. Dasgupta, S. A. Marglin and A. K. Sen, New York: United Nations.

US Congress, Joint Economic Committee (1980) *The Underground Economy*, Hearing, 96 Cong., 1 sess., Washington, DC: US Government Printing Office.

US Dept. of Commerce, Bureau of the Census (1981) *General Report on Industrial Organization. 1977 Enterprise Statistics*, Washington, DC: US Government Printing Office.

——, Bureau of Economic Analysis (1982) 'Revised Estimates of the National Income and Product Accounts', *Survey of Current Business*, 62(7) July: 4 – 136.

Usher, Dan (1968) *The Price Mechanism and the Meaning of National Income Statistics*, Oxford: Clarendon Press.

Vernon, Raymond (1966) 'Comprehensive Model-building in the Planning Process: The Case of the Less Developed Economies', *Economic Journal*, 76(301): 57 – 69.

Vining, Rutledge (1949) 'Methodological Issues in Quantitative Economics: Koopmans on the Choice of Variables to be Studied and of Methods of Measurement', 'A Rejoinder', *Review of Economics and Statistics*, 31: 77 – 94. Reprinted in *The Scientific Papers of Tjalling C. Koopmans*, Berlin, Heidelberg, New York: Springer-Verlag, 1970, pp. 132 – 48, 157 – 63.

von Mises, Ludwig (1962) *The Ultimate Foundations of Economic Science: An Essay on Method*, Princeton, NJ, etc.: Van Nostrand.

von Neumann, John (1963) 'The General and Logical Theory of Automata', *Collected Works*, vol. V, *Design of Computers, Theory of Automata and Numerical Analysis*, Oxford, London, etc.: Pergamon Press, pp. 288 – 328.

—— and H. H. Goldstine (1963) 'Numerical Inverting of Matrices of High Order', in John von Neumann, *Collected Works*, vol. V, *Design of Computers, Theory of Automata and Numerical Analysis*, Oxford, London, etc.: Pergamon Press, pp. 479 – 572.

Warford, Jeremy J. (1971) 'The Role of Economics in Municipal Water Supply: Theory and Practice', *Memorandum of the Public Utilities*

Dept., Washington, DC: World Bank.

Weizenbaum, Joseph [1976] *Computer Power and Human Reason, From Judgment to Calculation*, San Francisco: W. H. Freeman.

Wernecke, Diane (1979) 'Measuring Economic Hardship in the Labor Market', *American Economic Review*, 69(2): 43 – 53.

Wiener, Norbert (1964) *God and Golem, Inc.: A Comment on Certain Points Where Cybernetics Impinges on Religion*, Cambridge, Mass.: MIT Press; London: Chapman and Hall.

Willes, Mark H. (1981) 'Rational Expectations as a Counterrevolution', in Daniel Bell and Irving Kristol (eds), *The Crisis in Economic Theory*, New York: Basic Books, pp. 81 – 96.

Williamson, Oliver E. (1981) 'The Modern Corporation: Origins, Evolution, Attributes', *Journal of Economic Literature*, 19(4): 1537 – 68.

Wilson, George W. (1979) 'The Concept of Capital and its Role in Economic Growth', in Gehrels, Oliver and Wilson (eds), *Essays in Economic Analysis*, Bloomington, Ind.: Indiana University Press, pp. 192 – 215.

World Bank (1976) *World Tables 1976*, Baltimore, Md and London: Johns Hopkins University Press for the World Bank.

Worswick, G. D. N. (1972) 'Is Progress in Economic Science Possible?' Presidential Address to Section F of the British Association, 2 Sept. 1971, *Economic Journal*, 82(325): 73 – 86.

Yaffey, M. (1971) 'Balance of Payments of a Developing Country: Tanzania', quoted on p. 32 of John Loxley, 'The Behavior of the Tanzania Money Supply 1966 – 1970', ERB Paper 71.3, Economic Research Bureau, University of Dar es Salaam, mimeo.

Young, Crawford (1978) 'Zaire: The Unending Crisis', *Foreign Affairs*, 57(1): 169 – 85.

Zarnowitz, Victor (1978) 'How Have Forecasts Worked? On the Accuracy and Properties of Recent Macroeconomic Forecasts', *American Economic Review*, 68(2): 313 – 19.

Zinman, John (1978) *Reliable Knowledge: An exploration of the grounds for belief in science*, Cambridge, London, etc.: Cambridge University Press.

Index

abortion, 24
accounting, imprecision of, 14
accuracy: definition, 1 – 2, 13;
    political factors, 16; set by
    least accurate component, 117,
    134 – 8; understanding limits of, 1,
    8, 13 – 16, 117
Adams, Ernest W., 24
addition with significant digits, 137
Adelman, Irma, x
Adelman, M. A., 90 – 1
algorithms, 124, 126
American Agricultural Economics
    Association, 15, 33
American Economic Association, viii,
    72, 122
American Economic Review, analysis
    of articles, 122
analytical insight, *see* judgement
anti-bads, 58
Argentina, 47
Aristotle, 1, 27, 133
Arrow, Kenneth, 3, 10, 17, 30, 99, 126
artificial intelligence, 88, 125
as-if approach, 5
Ash, J. C. K., 72
Asian Development Bank, 107
Augustine, Saint, 42, 82

balance of payments, 62 – 8, 120;
    current account discrepancy, 63 – 4,
    120

banking system, 40
Barco, Virgilio, vii
barter sector, 51
Bauer, P. T., 77, 112
Baumol, William, 91
behaviour, motive forces of, 82
behavioural theory of rational choice,
    93
Bell, Carolyn Shaw, 34
Bennett, Amanda, 93
Bernouilli, J., 23
bias in data, 12 – 16, 41
black economy, *see* underground
    economy
Black, Eugene, 96
Black, Max, 25
Blaug, Mark, 5, 100
Bolivia, 50
Bonnen, James T., 15, 33, 44
border prices, 102 – 3
borderline member of class, 25, 26
Borders, William, 46
Bos, H. C., 107
Boskin, Michael J., 119
Boston Snow Theory, 5 – 6
bounded rationality, 84, 93
British Institute of Management, 45
Brunner, Karl, 72
Bruton, Henry J., 36
Burma, 67
business investment: function, 77; in
    non-material goods, 113 – 14

Cairncross, Alec, 17, 73
Cape Cod, 2, 50
capital, 75, 76, 106 – 16;
    confusion over capital goods =
    capital, 107 – 8, 114; formation as
    central in theory, 107, 114;
    income, 119; movements, 62,
    65 – 8; opportunity cost of, 102;
    – output ratio, 21, 107, 111; stock,
    107
Carter, President J., 122
centralized planning, 127
centrally planned economies, 46, 48,
    87, 95, 97 – 9
certainty, 3, 133
Ceylon, 67
Chandler, Alfred D., Jr, 89
change, in structure, 30, 33;
    agriculture, 33 – 4; family, 34;
    financial institutions, 39 – 40;
    markets, 36 – 7; money, 37 – 9;
    unemployment, 34 – 5
Chenery, Hollis, 32, 107
China, 16
Christ, Carl F., 15
Chunking, 88 – 9, 124
Citicorp, 40
Clague, Christopher, 95
Clark, Colin, law of government
    fiscal ceiling, 21
Clark William, ix
class, definition, 25
Collum, Maria, x
Colombia, 50
commodity: definition, 28;
    measurement of output, 42;
    statistics, 28 – 9
comprehensive development plans,
    107
comprehensive planning models,
    75 – 7
construct, 78
consumer: basic postulate of
    behaviour, 80 – 2; confidence,
    83; theory of, 80 – 6
consumption, 52; relation to
    disposable income, 83

corporation, 87, 89 – 97; as
    battleground, 95; managers,
    89 – 96; policy objectives, 91 – 4;
    takeovers, 93, 111
correctness, *see* accuracy
correlations and causal relationships,
    5
cost – benefit analysis, 29, 98 – 105
Courant, Paul N., 61
Cowles Commission, 15
crime, 49 – 50
Cyert, Richard M., 90
Czechoslovakia, 48

Dasgupta, A. K., 2
Davidson, Paul, 21
de V. Graaff, J., 101
decision: elements, 126; model, 130;
    problem, 126; techniques, 125 – 6
defensive goods, 58
Delphi technique, 130
Denison, Edward F., 43
deposit-sweeping accounts, 38
determining outcomes, 127
determinism, 89
deterministic theory, competitive and
    oligopolistic markets, 31
development: aid statistics
    discrepancies, 64, 110; pattern
    study, 32; plans, 129
Devons, Ely, 120
Dewey, John, 12
DeWulf, Luc, 64
direct contact with reality as data, 132
disturbance, *see* random errors
diversification, virtue of, 129
division with significant digits, 136
Dorfman, Robert, 31, 42, 121
Dorn, Pamela, x
Dow, Greg, 61
Drucker, Peter, 35, 132
drunk and street light, 115
dual economy, *see* underground
    economy
Dunlop, John T., 103 – 4

Easterlin, R. A., 60

Easterlin paradox, 60
Eastern Europe, 16, 46, 48, 87, 95, 97
econometric practice, 9
econometrics, 9, 15, 71, 77 – 8
economic analysis, 117, 121 – 5; data,
   117 – 21, 123; interpretation, 2;
   laws, 21; management
   effectiveness, 133; policy since
   World War II,
   133; reality as dynamic process,
   117; training, vii, ix; welfare,
   57 – 61, 98 – 101, 104 – 5
economics: as art, vii, 121 – 2; as
   science, vii, 121 – 2; as uncertain
   truth, 131; of measurement, 118
economics, valid practice in: analysis,
   forecasts and model-making,
   21 – 2, 30, 74, 78 – 9, 86, 96 – 7,
   121 – 5;
   cost – benefit analysis, 105;
   definition of investment, 113 – 15;
   international comparisons, 54 – 7;
   national accounts, 53 – 4, 61;
   policy-making, 21 – 2, 125 – 33;
   preparation and use of data, 7,
   8 – 9, 60 – 1, 74, 117 – 21; theory-
   making, 5 – 6, 32
Economist, 16, 18, 39, 47, 48
education and training rates of
   return, 103 – 4
effective procedures, 124, 126
efficiency analysis, 101
energy, 128 – 9
errors: in calculation, 10; in
   economics, 12 – 16; in parameters,
   10; in rounding, 10 – 11; inherent in
   measurement and computation,
   8 – 11; political – economic, 70
estimates, 28, 105
Ethiopia, vii, viii
evaluating economic position, 120
excluded middle, law of, 27
expectations, 20 – 1
expense accounts, 45 – 6
exponential problems, 126
external benefits and costs, 31, 58 – 9,
   101 – 2, 105

Fabricant, Solomon, 44
fallacy of affirming a consequent,
   76 – 7
false assumptions in economics, 4 – 6
family farm, 33
family, planning of expenditure, 110
family, typical, 34
farm population, 33
Federal Reserve Board, ix, 37, 49, 128
Feldstein, Martin, 35
financial institution concept, 40
financing physical capital as key to
   development, 107 – 8
fine-tuning, 73 – 4, 126 – 7
firm, theory of, 80, 86 – 97
Fisherian definition of investment,
   113
flow of funds, 49, 119
food and fibre sector, 15
Forbes, 17
forecasting the present, 17 – 18
forecasts: 5, 17 – 22, 84, 89, 128 – 9;
   from consumer attitudes, 84;
   money supply, 18; population, 18;
   risks, 84 – 5; the present, 17 – 18;
   US budget, 18 – 19; US GNP,
   72 – 3
Fortune, 51
France, 16, 70
Friedman, Milton, 4 – 5
fudging, 73 – 4

Garner, Robert, 96
Gauss, C. F. W., 23, 120, 135
Geertz, Clifford, 41
General Electric, 40
General Motors, 96
Georgescu-Roegen, Nicholas, 7,
   20 – 1, 79, 80, 117
German postwar recovery, 112
Ghana, 109 – 10
GNP, *see* national accounts
GNP per capita, use of, 53
Goedel, Kurt, 1
Goldstine, H. H., 9 – 10
Goodhart, Charles, 39
Gordon, Lester, ix

government, impact on models, 70, 71
grants economy, 99
Green Revolution and investment, 110 – 11
Greene, Richard, 14
Griliches, Zvi, 106 – 7
group behaviour, 85 – 6
growth in developed countries, explanation, 109
growth models, 74 – 7
Guinea, 53
Guisinger, Stephan, 102 – 3

Hahn, F. H., 20
Hall, R. E., 125
Harberger, Arnold, 36
Harrod – Domar model, 107
Harvard Institute of International Development, ix
Hayek, F. A., 3, 86
health: benefits of piped water, 103; care, 29; factor in growth, 109; services, 43
Hedrick, Charles L., 90
Helleiner, Gerald K., 66
Hendry, David F., 5
Herman, Edward S., 87
heuristics, 124, 125 – 6
Hicks, John, 1, 21, 36 – 7, 58
hidden economy, *see* underground economy
hierarchical levels, 88 – 9
hierarchy of expenditures and returns proposal, 112
high technology industries, 111 – 12, 113 – 14
Hirsch, Fred, 59
historians and quantification, 120 – 1
Hogg, Vincent, x
holism, 87
human capital, 108, 112
Hungary, 48
Hutchison, T. W., ix, 7, 62

IBM and investment, 111
ideas, reception of, viii

ignorance, effects of, 40 – 1
imperfectly observable variables in public finance, 119
inaccuracy: in economic data, 12 – 16; in forecasting, 16 – 22; in knowledge of present, 17 – 18
income: capital, 119; in-kind, 45 – 6; tax evasion, 47 – 9
incrementalism, 126 – 7
index numbers, 28, 32, 44
India, 16, 57
individual: definition, 24; economic behaviour, theory of, 80 – 6
Indonesia, 36, 67
inflation, theory, 31
information, search for, 41
Inland Revenue, 47
input – output models, 79, 119
Institute of Labor and Industrial Relations, 51
intangible capital assets, 108
intelligence as comprehensive and multi-level, 125
Inter-American Development Bank, 107
inter-personal comparisons, 100
internal rate of return, 112
Internal Revenue Service (IRS), 47 – 50
international comparison of real products, 54 – 7
International Monetary Fund, 63, 64
intertwining of objectives and policies, 126 – 7
intra-personal comparisons, 99 – 100
investment, 52, 75 – 6, 106 – 16; as driving force, 107, 114; estimated from trade figures, 66 – 8, 75 – 6, 114; expenditure for future income flow, 111 – 15; expenditure on material capital, 106 – 8; Fisherian definition, 113; function, 77, 107
isomorphic to reality, isomorphism, 4, 69, 124
Italy, 16, 47, 49, 70

Jamaica, 50

James, William, viii
Japan, 46, 70, 112
Johnson, H. G., 112
judgement, analytical insight, 74, 78,
    121, 123, 125, 132 – 3
Juster, F. Thomas, 43, 61

Kaldor, N., 117
Kamarck, Andrew M., 36, 109
Kantorovich, L. V., 97
Katona, George, 83 – 4
Katsenelinboigen, Aron, 97
Katz, Daniel, 95
Keats, John, 116
Kenya, 76
Keynes, John Maynard, 2, 69, 83, 108
King, Benjamin B., x, 119
Klein, Frederick C., 51, 52
Klein, Lawrence, 73
Knight, Frank, 85
Koerner, Stephan, 13, 24
Koopmans, Tjalling C., vii, 72,
    80 – 1, 121
Kornai, Janos, 95
Koten, John, 92
Kravis, Irving B., 56, 102
Kunreuther, Howard, 84 – 5
Kuznets, Simon, 58, 78, 79, 109

labour force, US, 34
labour supply function, 77 – 8
land reform, 127
Lanzillotti, Robert F., 92, 93
Laspeyre index, 32
Lawson, Tony, 125
Leibenstein, Harvey, 85, 89, 94 – 5,
    102
Leibnitz, 23
Leontief, Wassily, viii, 33, 79, 122
Letiche, John M., ix
Liber, Paul, 123
limitative results, 1
Lindblom, Charles E., 127
linear programming, 125
Lipsey, Robert E., 102
Little, I. M. D., 98, 100 – 2, 104
Loeb, Martin, 97

logico-mathematical reasoning, 6
loose concepts, 25 – 9, 32 – 5, 123;
    . reasoning with, 27
Lowe, Adolph, 7, 19
Lowenthal, Martin D., 51

M1, M2 – M5, 37 – 9
macroeconomic models, 69 – 79;
    record of performance, 71 – 3
Magat, Wesley, A., 97
Maisel, Sherman, J., 18, 128
Malaya, 67
mantissa, 11, 135
Margenau, Henry, 24
marginal utility, 85
margins of error, 8, 24, 41, 140
margins of precision, 7, 26, 120, 131;
    see also precision
market: concept, 36 – 7; price, 40 – 1
Marris, Robin, 87, 91
Marshall, Alfred, 2, 27 – 8
Marshall Plan, 130
Marx, Karl, 21; law of falling real
    wage, 21
Mason, Edward S., ix, 77, 87
material capital goods, 106 – 8
material goods, Hirsch definition, 59
mathematical understanding and
    precision, 120, 135
mathematics in economics, 2 – 3, 69
Mayer, Thomas, ix, 9
McKinley, John K., 129
measurement, 8 – 10, 23 – 4, 135;
    capability in economics, 123 – 4;
    error, 13; of expectations, 20 – 1;
    of output, 42 – 54
mechanics model for economics, 7, 21
Meier, Gerald M., ix
Menger, Karl, 20
Merill Lynch Pierce Fenner and
    Smith, 40
meteorology, 22
Michael, Walther P., 62
microeconomics, 80 – 97
Minnich, Elizabeth Kamarck, x
Mirrlees, J. A., 101 – 2, 104
Mishan, E. J., 98, 101, 106

models, 4, 6 – 7, 9 – 10, 29 – 31, 69 – 79; 122, 124, 132; and crime, 46, 49 – 51; and money supply, 39; as games or science fiction, 6, 117; decision-making, 126, 130; elegant, 122; expressing likelihood of approximating reality, 132; growth, 74 – 7; in applied mathematics, 9; in determining a solution, 123; in engineering, 123; in physics, 4, 7, 132; in Rational Expectations, 19 – 20; macro-economic record of performance, 71 – 3

money supply measures, 37 – 9

Montaigne, M. E. de, 80

Morgan, Theodore, ix, 67, 106, 112

Morgenstern, Oskar, 13, 15, 53, 106

Moss, Milton, 43

muddling through, 127

Mueller, Dennis C., 87, 91

multinational corporations intrafirm trade, 66

multiplication with significant digits, 136

national accounts, 42 – 61, 106, 119, 120, 132; and welfare, 57 – 61; distorted by controls, 66; in less developed countries, 52 – 4; in real terms, 30, 54 – 7; reinforcing, 119

National Bureau of Economic Research (NBER), 43, 62, 72, 124 – 5

National Semiconductor, 111

Naya, Seiji, 67

negative capability, 116, 124

Nelson, Richard A., 117

neutral member of class, 25, 26

new public finance, 119

Nigeria, 53

noise in statistical data, 4, 11, 117, 119, 136, 140

non-marketed production, *see* subsistence

NOW accounts, 38

number, meaning of, 135

objective function, 126

Oedipus effect, 20

off-the-book, 46, 51

Official Development Assistance, 64, 110

oil sector, 128 – 9

Okigbo, Pius, 53

oligopoly, theory, 31

Olivieri, René, ix

operational conclusions, 116 – 33

operations research, 125

optimizing, maximizing, 82, 84, 90 – 6; models, 78; objective function, 126

Organization for Economic Co-operation and Development (OECD), 39, 45, 48 – 9, 50, 63 – 4, 72, 110

Paasche index, 32

Papageorgiou, Demetrios, 102 – 3

parallel economy, *see* underground economy

parameters, errors in, 10; unpredictable change in, 19; political influences, 19

Pareto, Vilfredo, 3, 20; decision, 131; improvement, 101; law of inequality of income, 21; optimality as normative, 131

Park, Thae, S., 48

Penner, Rudy G., 19

perfect competition and social benefit, 98

Perkins, Dwight H., ix

Perks, 45 – 6, 91

Philippines, 67

Phillips curve, 28

physical capital goods, definition, 106

physics, 4, 7, 21, 123, 132

Pile, Sir William, 47

planning process, importance of, 129

Policy instruments, 126; strategy, 128

policy-making, 125 – 33; in small steps or incrementally, 127; with imprecision and ignorance, 127 – 8

pollution and national accounts, 58 – 9; economics of, 31, 58 – 9, 99
Popper, Karl, 122
population projections, 18
positional goods, 59 – 60
possible error, definition, 135
poverty of resources for data improvement, 118
Prais, S. J., 30, 42
precisely correct answers, futility and dangers of, 130
precision: definition, 1 – 2; and mathematical understanding, 23, 120, 135; as self-deception, 1 – 2, 54, 79, 109, 114 – 15, 120; in economics and physics, 7; need to understand, 8; spurious, vii, 1 – 2, 8, 14, 23, 54, 114 – 15, 120, 139; *see also* margins of precision
predicate, 25
predictability, 89; and changes in people, 19 – 20, 129
prediction criterion, 4 – 6
predictions, *see* forecasts
Prest, A. R., 53
prices: deflators, 44; elements of imprecision, 29, 102 – 3
probability, 20 – 1; analysis, 140; assessment in decisions, 130, 132; density function, 140
production function, 90 – 3
profit-maximization, 5, 90 – 6
prohibition, 50
project analysis, *see* cost – benefit analysis
propensity to import, 68
propensity to save, 107
pseudo-optimizing models, 78
pseudo-problems, 122
pseudo-science, 6
purchasing power parities, 55 – 7
pure number, 135, 136

qualitative calculus, 119
quantification, 7; need to understand, 8, 9, 114
quantitative calculus, 119

quantum mechanics, 1

random errors, 15, 30
ratchet principle, 97
Rational Expectations, 19 – 20
reality and change, 32 – 4; relationship to theory, 24 – 6
recession, objective formula to determine, 124 – 5
recognition of limitations widening policy sphere, 131
reductionism, 87
redundancy, need for, 126, 129
Reich-Ranicki, Marcel, 16
relative error, definition, 135
repos, 38
reserves, need for, 129
Reynolds, Lloyd G., 61, 78
rigour, relationship to precision, 7
Rivlin, Alice, 43
Robbins, Lionel, 80 – 1
Robinson, Joan, 108, 112
rolling plans, 129
Routh, Guy, ix
Rudd, Ernest, 13 – 14
Ruggles, Nancy D., 53
Ruggles, Richard, 44

sailing as metaphor for policy, 128
Salamon, Gerald L., 91
sampling errors, 8, 14, 118
Samuels, Warren J., 131
Samuelson, Paul, 21, 131
satisficing, 84
Schmedtje, Jochen K., 102
Schoeffler, Sidney, 7
scholasticism: economics, philosophy, engineering, 122 – 3
Schumpeter, Joseph A., 117
science and quantification, 8 – 9
science fiction and economics, 6, 98, 117
scientific notation, 11, 135
scientific procedures, requirements, 9
Scitovsky, Tibor, 82 – 3, 91, 101
Sears, Roebuck, 40
second-best, theory of, 100-1

Seers, Dudley, 52 – 3
self-employed, 47, 119
Sen, Amartya, 99
sensitivity analysis, 139
services: measurement, 29, 42 – 4;
    price, 29
Shackle, G. L. S., 16
shadow prices, 101
Shourie, Arun, 75 – 7
Shubik, Martin, 13
signal, and noise, 11, 117, 119
significant digits, 11, 54, 117, 124,
    134 – 40
Simon, Herbert A., 84, 93, 126
Singapore, 67
sketch, 78
Slovic, Paul, 84 – 5
Smith, E. Dan, 91
Smith, John S., 62
Smith, Vernon, 113
Smithies, Arthur, ix
Smyth, D. J., 72
Social Accounting Matrix (SAM), 119
social analysis, 101 – 2, 104 – 5
social economy, 51 – 2
Social objectives and cost – benefit
    analysis, 101 – 2, 104 – 5
Social Science Research Council, 72
social sectors, 103 – 4
social welfare function, 98 – 9
sorites sophism, 25
Soviet Union, 16, 46, 48, 87, 112, 127
Spain, 16
spillover effects, 31, 58 – 9, 99, 105
spurious precision, *see* precision
Squire, Lynn, 101 – 2
statistical magic, 120
statistics as a two-person game, 15
Stevenson, Alexander, x
Stewart, Frances, 104
Stewart, I. G., 53
Stigler, George, 40 – 1
Stiglitz, Joseph E., 119
stochastic element, 15, 29 – 30
Stolper, Wolfgang F., 77
Stone, Christopher, 90
Stone, Lawrence, 120 – 1

Stone, Richard, 30, 42
Stout, Russell, 126
Streeten, Paul, ix, 3, 66, 77, 112
Strumpel, Burkhard, 84
sub-optimization, 3
submerged/subterranean economy,
    see underground economy
subsistence output, 44 – 5, 52
subtraction with significant digits, 137
supply-side economics, 17 – 18
surprise, need to provide for
    probability of, 129

target goods, 85
Taylor, Lance, 32
technical cooperation/assistance, 104,
    110
tendencies, *see* trends
Thailand, 57, 67
theory, 3, 6 – 7, 31 – 2; effective or
    useful as equivalent to
    deterministic, 31 – 2; functions of,
    5 – 6; of inflation, 31; relation to
    reality, 24 – 6
Thomas, Lewis, 116
Thurow, Lester C., 31 – 2, 77 – 8
Tinbergen, Jan, 107
Tintner, Gerhard, 79
Titmuss, Richard M., 45
Todaro, Michael, 36
trade statistics problems, 64 – 8, 75
transaction costs, 40 – 1, 84
transfer prices and trade data, 66 – 7
trends as best representation of
    reality, 22, 128, 131 – 2
Triplett, Jack E., 29, 83, 118
true value, 2, 13, 23 – 4, 28, 41, 135

UK Ministry of Agriculture, 47
UN standard investment definition,
    108
uncertainty: behaviour under, 84 – 5;
    judgement of, 140; of future,
    16 – 22; policy under, 126 – 33
underground economy, 16, 45 – 52
unemployment, 27, 34 – 6, 51, 120; in
    less developed countries, 35 – 6

unexplained residual factor, 109
UNIDO, 102
University of Michigan, 51
unquantifiable elements, 3, 120
Upper Volta, 109
US Bureau of Census, vii
US Chamber of Commerce, 50
US Congress, 47, 50
US Department of Commerce, 49, 50
US dollar, 39
US Government Accounting Office, 34, 51
US National Petroleum Council, 128
US oil imports projections, 128 – 9
US Securities and Exchange Commission, 91
Usher, Dan, 57 – 8
utopia, 98, 99

validity, 3
van der Tak, Herman G., 101 – 2
Vernon, Raymond, ix
von Neumann, John, 7, 8 – 10

Walters, A. A., 77
Ward, William, x
Warford, Jeremy, 103
water supply projects, 103
Wayne State University, 51
Weizenbaum, Joseph, 6

welfare economics, 98 – 101
Whitehead, Alfred N., 116
Wiener, Norbert, 8 – 9
Willes, Mark H., 20
Williamson, Oliver E., 91
willingness to spend, factor in predictions, 84
Wilson, George W., 106
Winter, Sidney G., 117
Woods, George, 96
working party, 130
World Bank, viii, 63, 79, 103 – 4, 107 – 8, 109, 112 – 13; *Atlas*, 55; cost – benefit methodology, 101 – 2; Economics Department, 55, 96
World Development Indicators, 53 – 4
world neither all order nor chaos, 127 – 8
World Tables, vii
Wriston, Walter, 40

X-inefficiency, 94 – 7, 102

Yamey, B. S., 112
Youker, Robert, x
Young, Crawford, 65

Zaire, 51, 65
Zarnowitz, Victor, 73
Zinman, John, 4, 73, 123